Book 2

Edited by Thomas A. Nummela

Consultants

Jennifer AlLee, Steve Christopher, Tom Doyle, Roger Howard, Joan Lilley, Jay Reed, Tom Rogers, Carolyn Sims, and Roger Sonnenberg

Contributors for the Bible Studies

Steve Christopher, Joan Lilley, Jay Reed, Carolyn Sims, and Roger Sonnenberg

Contributors for the Plays

Jennifer AlLee, Steve Christopher, Mark Eiken, Roger Howard, Joan Lilley, Dean Nadasdy, Carolyn Sims, Roger Sonnenberg

Cynthia Anderson, assistant to the editor

Cover photos, H. Armstrong Roberts, Inc.

Your comments and suggestions concerning the material are appreciated. Please write to Editor, Youth Bible Studies, Concordia Publishing House, 3558 S. Jefferson Avenue, St. Louis, MO 63118-3968.

Unless otherwise indicated, Scripture quotations are taken from the HOLY BIBLE, NEW INTERNATIONAL VERSION®. NIV®. Copyright © 1973, 1978, 1984 by International Bible Society. Used by permission of Zondervan Publishing House. All rights reserved.

Quotations marked KJV are from the King James or Authorized Version of the Bible.

Copyright © 1995 Concordia Publishing House
3558 South Jefferson Avenue, St. Louis, MO 63118-3968
Manufactured in the United States of America

All rights reserved. Except for the student pages and skits, which the purchaser may reproduce for Christian education or church program use, no part of this publication may be reproduced, stored in a retrieval system, or transmitted, in any form or by any means, electronic, mechanical, photocopying, recording, or otherwise, without the prior written permission of Concordia Publishing House.

1 2 3 4 5 6 7 8 9 10   04 03 02 01 00 99 98 97 96 95

Contents

Introduction ... 4

Friends and Peers

1. I Can Help! ... 6
Student Page 1
Power Play 1: "Busy, Busy, Busy"

2. The Price of Popularity ... 13
Student Pages 2 and 3
Power Play 2: "Popularity's Price"

3. When Friends Make Me Choose ... 20
Student Pages 4 and 5
Power Play 3: "From My Point of View"

Priorities in Life

4. What Will I Do with My Life? ... 27
Student Page 6
Power Play 4: "Dialog with God"

5. How Will I Know When I've Got It Made? ... 33
Student Pages 7 and 8
Power Play 5: "Quality Control"

Sexuality and Sanctity of Life

6. Special People, Special Purpose ... 40
Student Page 9
Power Play 6: "The 'In' Crowd"

7. Who Values Life? ... 46
Power Play 7: "Decisions"

8. God Created Sex! ... 52
Student Page 10
Power Play 8: "Sizzlin' Sam's Roller Coaster Ride"

Media and Leisure

9. Me First? ... 58
Student Page 11
Power Play 9: "The Youth Group That Lost (and Gained) Everything"

10. My Music—To God's Glory! ... 65
Power Play 10: "Music and Its Influence"

11. Whom Do You Admire Most and Why? ... 70
Student Page 12
Power Play 11: "Who's Your Hero?"

12. Peace of Mind in Violent Times ... 75
Student Page 13
Power Play 12: "Violence"

Introduction

You are holding one of two books of 12 skit-based Bible studies for high school youth. These books focus on some of the most powerful texts of Scripture. These studies were written to assist young people in their understanding of how the power of God's Word works in their daily lives—what we frequently call sanctification.

Each study includes a skit—a power play—designed for performance in class to provoke discussion or illustrate the application of Scripture to real life. The scripts for these plays can be copied for your use. The power plays can be read in class with a minimum of advance preparation, or they can be assigned in advance and staged in a more elaborate manner.

A book of devotional studies for adults and youth has been prepared to supplement these studies—*Power Words: Devotional Studies for Youth Bible Study Leaders* (CPH 1995, stock number 20-2629). It follows the arrangement and scriptural texts in *Power Plays, Books 1 and 2*. These devotions provide excellent in-depth preparation for the person who leads these studies. They could also be used for personal or group study apart from *Power Plays*.

About Power Plays

God provides power in the lives of His people. The power of the Gospel saves us as Paul says in Romans 1:16: "I am not ashamed of the Gospel, because it is the power of God for the salvation of everyone who believes: first for the Jew, then for the Gentile." God also provides the continuing power of our new life of faith. "I have been crucified with Christ and I no longer live, but Christ lives in me. The life I live in the body, I live by faith in the Son of God, who loved me and gave Himself for me" (Galatians 2:20).

This power for daily living, our sanctification, is frequently misunderstood or underestimated. Many clearly and correctly ascribe their salvation to God's action alone but credit their growth in discipleship, or lack thereof, to their own efforts—in misplaced pride or despair.

The power of Christ at work in us through the Holy Spirit enables us to grow in faith and in good works, which are the evidence of faith (James 2:18). There is nurturing power in the Gospel, the good news of forgiveness through the suffering and death of Christ. We receive power as we hear God's Word and share in the Sacraments He has provided. The Gospel frees us from the guilt and enslavement of past sin. Each day it offers us new strength to live according to God's will. The Gospel is that kind of power.

This book and its companion, *Power Plays, Book 1* (CPH 1995 20-2627), explore 24 issues in life. In each issue young people will see God's powerful Word at work, granting forgiveness and growth in discipleship.

The Studies

The 12 studies in this book are grouped according to topic, but they can be used in any order.

The topic, objectives, and outline of the lesson are summarized on the first page of each study. Nearly every study assumes the presence of a chalkboard or marker board or newsprint and markers in the classroom. Newsprint easel pads are available in most office supply stores. Roll ends of newsprint are frequently available for no or low cost from your local newspaper office. Any other materials needed or suggested for the study are listed in the table headed "This Study at a Glance." Occasionally, advance preparation is vital to an activity. Watch for "starred" activities in the "This Study at a Glance"; check those activities for preparation instructions.

Some, but not all, studies have one or two reproducible student pages following the leaders guide pages for use during the study. The leader should prepare enough copies of these pages before class so that each student can have one.

The Power Plays

Also following the leaders guide pages of each study is a two-page power play. Each play takes 5–10 minutes to read and discuss in class and is the basis for part of the study. The leader should make enough copies of the script for each part.

Although the plays can be read in class with a minimum of preparation, they will have greater impact with advance preparation. Consider assigning the performance to an appropriate number of students a week or more in advance. Instruct them to obtain the necessary props, practice, and if possible memorize the script in preparation for the performance.

Most of the plays can be performed in very little space. If a "theater" space (auditorium, stage, or worship area) is available, that would be even better. Some of the plays may be useful also in other settings. Consider presenting them for other classes or for the congregation as a part of the worship service.

God's Power at Work

God will be at work in the study of these power plays. His grace will supply strength and new life to your students just as He promises. God bless.

1

I Can Help!

Focus

Because of His great love, Christ laid down His life for us. While we were yet sinners, Jesus died for us. As our friend, He has helped us through our biggest problem—sin—and continues to help us in all other problems in life. Through His power at work in us we extend His friendship to those around us.

Objectives

By the power of Christ at work through His Word and Spirit the students will

1. identify frustrations in helping friends deal with problems;
2. learn to listen instead of "giving advice";
3. gain strength and support from God's Word to be a friend to others;
4. develop a plan to help a friend with a problem.

A Powerful Word for the Leader

For additional perspective on this topic a devotional study is available for the leader. It is "Love Me, Love My Problems?" unit 2, study 1, found in *Power Words: Devotional Studies for Youth Bible Study Leaders*, CPH 20-2629.

This Study at a Glance

Activity	Time	Materials
Opener	15 minutes	
Busy, Busy, Busy	10 minutes	Three copies of power play 1
God's Word	10 minutes	Bibles
*Listening Tips	15 minutes	Copies of student page 1 for each student; one copy of "Problems" for every three students anticipated in class
Closing	10 minutes	

*Advance preparation or special supplies required.

Opener

Form groups of three. Then share the following hypothetical problem with the class. Direct each group to briefly list on scrap paper several ways to help in this situation.

> Your best friend comes in late from a party and is caught by his or her parents, gets grounded, and can't go to an upcoming party that you have been planning to attend together. What would you say? How would you help?

After a few minutes, allow members of each group to share their responses with the class. Summarize the responses on the board or on newsprint for all to see.

As the groups share, be alert to the kinds of responses they give, especially those that offer advice. It is likely that many of the responses will be in the form of advice. Point out to the students that while advice is always well-intended, it is not always helpful. Professional caregivers will usually refrain from giving advice. They will focus instead on intensive listening and feedback that allows clients to understand the situation clearly and helps them identify their own solutions. The ideal solutions come from the person with the problem. Advice from others allows the person with the problem to avoid coming up with the solution on his or her own.

Then say, "Listening is sometimes a difficult skill to learn and practice. It does not always come naturally, as we can see in the following situation."

Busy, Busy, Busy

Introduce the power play. At its conclusion, debrief with the following discussion questions.

1. Chris Fullup was "hard of hearing" in more ways than one. How could you tell? (He wasn't really listening to Joe at first.)

2. What specific obstacles interfered with Chris' ability to listen? (Doing two things at once, getting distracted, focusing on his own problems, e.g., "… tell *me* about lack of time.")

3. What other things might Chris have done to improve his ability to listen? (Answers will vary.)

4. What *did* Chris finally do? Why? (Chris finally gave his full attention to his friend. He was moved by his own recollection of God's Word—he heard the Gospel.)

God's Word

Sugggest to the class that the Word of God provides us with some suggestions of how we can best help our friends when they have a problem. Read or have a volunteer read 1 John 3:16–18. Then discuss the following questions.

1. What example of love is given in the passage? (Jesus Christ's perfect love.)

2. What does it mean to "lay down our lives for our brothers"? (Our "brothers" are fellow believers in Christ; "laying down our lives" will not often mean dying as Christ did, but it may involve a variety of ways in which we sacrifice ourselves, our time, or our possessions, for instance, sticking up for someone's reputation, offering assistance, showing compassion, or spending time in acts of service.)

3. How does it say we should love? ("With actions and in truth"—what we do speaks more loudly, more honestly, than what we say.)

4. Is that possible? (On our own it is not. Our sinful human nature will fail us. But in Christ we have forgiveness *and* power for new life. By God's grace, we have the Spirit of God working in us to help us.)

Listening Tips

Later in this section you will need a few copies of the "Problems" (boxed text). You will also need copies of student page 1.

Say, "Listening skills are one way in which we can show such love. We'll have a chance to practice listening skills in the next few moments. Let's look at a few tips on how to be a good listener

Problems

A—You are not doing well in a class you have to pass to graduate. The material is difficult, and you are not studying enough.

B—You have been asked out by a boy or girl you really like. You would like to go on the date but have been dating someone else regularly and don't want to hurt that relationship.

C—You need money and are offered an excellent part-time job that may lead to a full-time position, but it would mean quitting the basketball team and losing the chance of becoming a starter this coming season.

D—You are way behind in algebra and struggling to maintain a C. You don't know what to do because you don't like the teacher and are too proud to ask for help from your best friend, who is an excellent algebra student.

E—You really like a certain person at your school. You think (s)he might like you. You are afraid to ask the person out because you know your best friend wouldn't approve.

F—Your parents are fighting a lot these days. They seem to have a major argument every night. You want it to stop. You want them to get help, but you don't know how to approach them.

rather than just a giver of advice." Distribute copies of student page 1. Discuss the tips briefly, adding the following information.

1. *Use language that will encourage the person with the problem to open up.* Statements such as "I'm here to help" and "I'll be happy to assist you" make the individual feel comfortable in sharing the concern with you.

2. *Avoid asking probing questions* in the early stages of discussion. Questions for clarity are okay, but one should avoid interrogating the individual through multiple questions.

3. *Let the person have plenty of time* to share the problem. Allow the individual to take the time he or she needs. Let the person work at his or her speed, and not yours.

4. *Respond with statements that accurately reflect the person's feelings.* "You're really afraid of what your parents will do if they find out." "You are unsure of what choice you should make at this time."

5. *Avoid making judgments.* Statements such as "you know that is wrong," "you are really going to get it for that," and "I sure would not have done that" do not encourage the individual to continue to open up, even if the statements are true.

6. *Restate the problem.* "Sounds like you are really having difficulty communicating with your boy friend." "I sense that you are frustrated with your grade and are angry at the teacher because you think he was unfair."

7. *Avoid telling your autobiography.* Even though you may have been in a similar situation, the way you solved your problem will not necessarily be the best way in which another person should solve his or her problems.

8. *Let the person try to uncover ideas for solving the problem.* As he or she explores solutions, you may ask the person to narrow down ideas and to choose what he or she feels is best. The ideas should come from the person with the problem.

After reviewing the tips, form groups of three or four students. Instruct the groups to number themselves 1, 2, and 3 (and 4, if needed) in any way you choose (alphabetically, by height or age, randomly, etc.). Designate student 1 as the first "friend-in-need," student 2 as "listener," and the others as "observers." These roles will rotate. Give the friend-in-need one of the problems you have copied. As student 1 talks about the problem described, student 2 should practice listening using the tips discussed. After about a minute, the observer(s) will comment on how well the listening process went. Invite the observers to also be alert for signs that God's love is guiding the words and actions they hear.

Give a second situation to each group. This time student 2 will talk, student 3 will listen, and the others will observe. Repeat the pattern a third and fourth time, if possible, so that all students experience all roles.

Closing

Close with a prayer for friends who have problems. Ask students to share their prayer concerns and pray for those people and their needs.

Listening Tips

1. *Use language that will encourage the person with the problem to open up.*
2. *Avoid asking probing questions.*
3. *Let the person have plenty of time.*
4. *Respond with statements that accurately reflect the person's feelings.*
5. *Avoid making judgments.*
6. *Restate the problem.*
7. *Avoid telling your autobiography.*
8. *Let the person try to uncover ideas for solving the problem.*

Power Play 1

Busy, Busy, Busy

(Three copies of this script are needed.)

This is how we know what love is: Jesus Christ laid down His life for us. And we ought to lay down our lives for our brothers. If anyone has material possessions and sees his brother in need but has no pity on him, how can the love of God be in him? Dear children, let us not love with words or tongue but with actions and in truth. (1 John 3:16–18)

Characters

- JOE BURDENTON—a guy who is feeling overwhelmed by his problems and needs to talk to someone
- CHRIS FULLUP—a counselor who is really too busy to bother with Joe
- DORIS—a receptionist who helps Chris learn a lesson

Setting

A counselor's office adjacent to a receptionist's desk.

Props (Optional)

- CHRIS' office—desk, chair, side chair, telephone
- DORIS' office—desk, chair, computer or typewriter, telephone
- File folder
- Writing tablet and pencil

CHRIS (*seated at a desk, busily scribbling on a pad while talking on the telephone*): No, no, no, Benny. I told you, your cat does not have a grudge against you … No, they all look that way … Yes, his purr is a friendly sound. Now, give Ruffles a pet … That's right, Ben. Okay, I'll talk to you next week … Oh, and Benny? Bring the litter box this time. Thanks, bye. (*He hangs up and continues writing.*)

DORIS (*hits intercom*): Mr. Fullup, do you have that speech for the National Umbrella Twirlers Society for me to transcribe yet? I need to fax it to their chairman by 2:00 p.m.

CHRIS (*speaks to intercom*): Yes, Doris, just finishing the N.U.T.S. speech now. Come and get it—and bring me the file on Ben Fearly, would you please?

DORIS: Yes, sir. (*She stands, grabs a file folder from her drawer, and walks into CHRIS' office. He hands her a sheaf of papers; she hands him file folder and glances at her watch.*) Oh, a Mr. Joe Burdenton called to make an appointment with you, this morning, if possible. I told him to come by. He said he was a friend of yours, and it sounded urgent.

CHRIS (*sighs heavily; looks at paperwork*): Don't they all? Thanks, Doris, I'll try to squeeze him in. But hold my calls, will you? (*He begins leafing through file.*)

DORIS: Yes, sir. (*Sits at desk and begins typing speech.*)

JOE (*enters, looking very dejected with eyes down, shoulders hunched, hands in pockets. He walks up to DORIS' desk.*): Um, excuse me … I'm Joe Burdenton. I'm here to see Mr. Fullup.

DORIS (*smiles*): One moment, please. (*She hits intercom.*) Mr. Fullup, Joe Burdenton is here.

CHRIS (*looks at watch*): Okay, Doris, send him in. (*He shuffles more papers into file.*)

DORIS: You can go right in, Mr. Burdenton.

JOE: Uh, thanks. (*He enters CHRIS' office and extends his hand.*) Hi, Chris. Thanks for seeing me on such short notice.

CHRIS (*stands halfway up, shakes JOE'S hand once, sits back down quickly, and gestures JOE to side chair*): Hey, that's what friends are for, Joe. What's on your mind?

JOE (*sits*): Well, Chris, I really need to talk to someone, and of all of my friends, you can probably help me the most, so … (*shifts uncomfortably*) here I am.

CHRIS: I'm all ears … oops, just a second, Joe. (*He hits intercom.*) Doris, call my doctor and reschedule my hearing test for next week.

DORIS: Right away, Mr. Fullup.

CHRIS (*hits intercom*): Doris? Did you get that?

DORIS (*yelling*): Yes, sir!

CHRIS: All right, Joe, now where were we?

JOE: Um, well, there's a lot going on that I need to share with you. If this is not a good time, I can come back later …

CHRIS (*interrupts*): No, no, this is fine. What's up? (*He scribbles notes on a pad as JOE talks.*)

JOE: Well, where do I start? I guess … I guess it's all just hitting me at once. You see, I feel a need to spend more time in personal devotions—you know, prayer and reading my Bible and stuff. I've been kind of spiritually drained, and I know I need something, but it feels like there's so little time …

CHRIS (*interrupting*): Boy, tell *me* about lack of time, Joe!

JOE (*continues*): Yeh, well, most of my friends just wouldn't understand about things like faith and God. I've tried to live according to my faith more, but they act like I'm being really strange. In fact, some of my friends have started avoiding me.

CHRIS (*still scribbling notes, without looking up*): Yes, go on.

JOE: Well, my family's the same way. They don't understand. They think I'm crazy!

CHRIS: Well, Joe, "crazy" is such a harsh term. We prefer to say "rationally challenged."

JOE: Well, whatever you call it, it hurts when the accusation comes from your own family. I've talked to some of the people at my church too. All they seem to care about is whether or not I follow their rules. Why don't they seem to really care?

CHRIS: Uh, could you wait just one moment, Joe? (*He hits intercom.*) Doris, I just remembered that I'll need those notes typed up for the Bible class I'm supposed to lead tonight at First Church; also, call Pastor Paul and tell him I'll meet with him half an hour beforehand, please. Thanks. (*He looks up.*) Sorry, Joe … you were saying?

JOE: I guess what it boils down to is that I know I have to keep doing God's will for me. But it seems to involve a lot of trouble and suffering. I didn't expect that being faithful to God would be so hard. I'm not sure I can handle it.

CHRIS: I don't blame you, Joe. Even Jesus didn't want to (*he stops, suddenly struck with a thought*) … suffer … um, Joe, hold that thought just one more time. (*He hits intercom.*) Doris, please read back to me page 3, paragraph 2, of those Bible study notes for tonight.

DORIS: You mean right now?

CHRIS: Yes, yes, right now, please.

DORIS (*scans for page*): All right, Mr. Fullup … (*She finds the reference.*) Here it is: "Jesus must have felt a special urgency about His mission. His friends misunderstood Him, and some even deserted Him. His family accused Him of insanity. The church leaders of the day were only concerned with following the Law at the expense of love. He dreaded the suffering He faced on the cross. This opposition gives special impact to His words in Matthew 25: 'Whatever you did for one of the least of these brothers of Mine, you did for Me.' His human nature must have longed for the loving attention of friends. What amazing grace that He should give His life for those who rejected Him, so that they could be friends to others!"

CHRIS (*sits silently, looking at JOE. Finally …*): Thank you, Doris. That really helps me set my priorities straight today. Joe, let's get out of here.

JOE: But Chris, I don't understand …

CHRIS: We need someplace where there'll be no more interruptions. Let's take a walk. You deserve my undivided attention. (*CHRIS and JOE walk through DORIS' office to leave.*) Doris, take the rest of the day off. (*They exit.*)

DORIS (*turns off the computer and gets up to leave*): Yes, sir! (*She exits.*)

The Price of Popularity

This Study at a Glance

Activity	Time	Materials
What Is "Popularity?"	10 minutes	
Jesus' View	15 minutes	Bibles
Popular? or Blessed?	10 minutes	Bibles
Popularity's Price	15 minutes	Four copies of power play 2, copies of student page 2
Get Real!	5 minutes	Copies of student page 3
Closing	5 minutes	

What Is "Popularity?"

Brainstorm together as a large group: What makes someone popular? Say, "Think of the word *popular*. What comes to mind? What people? Which students in your high school? What makes them popular?" Write key words from student responses on newsprint or on the board for all to see. (Answers might include friendly, outgoing, helpful, great football player, pretty, or likeable.)

Jesus' View

Ask the students, individually or in small groups, to review Jesus' popularity by studying the following verses: Matthew 4:23–25; John 6:1–15; John 6:60–66; Mark 8:31–33; Matthew 21:1–11; Luke 23:13–25. After they have studied the verses, ask them to answer these questions.

1. In what three ways did Jesus minister to people according to Matthew 4:23? How did these things affect His popularity (vv. 24–25)? (Jesus' threefold ministry included teaching, preaching, and healing. This ministry brought Jesus great popularity—"large crowds" followed Him [v. 25].)

2. What does Jesus' response in John 6:14–15 tell us about His goals? (Jesus wanted no earthly kingship. He was a different sort of king—a king to redeem humankind from sin, death, and the power of the devil.)

Focus

The world, our flesh, and Satan would have us believe that nothing is more important than to be popular—to be noticed, accepted, included, invited! Though it is not sinful to be popular, it is sinful to value popularity more than our God and the morals and values He sets for our lives. We rejoice that Jesus Christ did not choose popularity but crucifixion, in order to redeem all people through His death. Because of His unpopularity, we become popular with God once again. Through Christ, God forgives the sins that separate us from Him and strengthens us to live in Him.

Objectives

By the power of Christ at work through His Word and Spirit the students will

1. identify the different things that make people popular;
2. confess that they have at times sought popularity with the world rather than with God;
3. give thanks to Jesus Christ for making them popular with God through His life, death, and resurrection.

A Powerful Word for the Leader

For additional perspective on this topic a devotional study is available for the leader. It is "Popularity," unit 2, study 2, found in *Power Words: Devotional Studies for Youth Bible Study Leaders*, CPH 20-2629.

3. When Jesus encountered trouble with the authorities, what did many of His followers do (John 6:66)? (They deserted Him.)

4. For Peter, what did popularity *not* include (Mark 8:31–33)? (Peter felt suffering and rejection had no place in Jesus' life.)

5. Contrast Jesus' popularity in Matthew 21:1–11 with the same in Luke 23:13–25. (Jesus' triumphal entry into Jerusalem was one of the last times the people gave Him honor and praise before His death. They hailed Him as king, as "the Son of David," as the One who had come to save them. Shortly afterward, some of the same people shouted, "Crucify Him!")

6. As you've studied these passages, what was Jesus' view of popularity? (Jesus cared little about popularity. He only wanted to do His Father's will—to redeem humankind with His own life, death, and resurrection.)

Popular? or Blessed?

Direct the students to Matthew 5:3–12. Draw a continuum on newsprint or on the board for all to see. Label the ends of the scale *9* and *1* or *high* and *low*. Remind the students of the popular people they identified. As you read each verse of the Bible passage and point out the extreme opposites in the list that follows, direct the students to imagine where they personally fall on the scale. Then ask where the popular people they've known might fit on the continuum.

> *Poor in spirit (needing God's grace) vs. spiritually proud and self-sufficient*
> *Those who mourn vs. those who enjoy the good things in life*
> *Meek (humble before God) vs. arrogant or proud*
> *Those who hunger and thirst for righteousness vs. those who do not seek God*
> *Merciful vs. the unforgiving*
> *Pure in heart vs. impure, sinful*
> *Peacemakers vs. quarrelsome*
> *Persecuted (for their faith in Christ) vs. nothing for which to be persecuted*

Invite the students to think for a moment about these questions. (Do not require sharing of personal responses, but you may have a few willing volunteers.) Did you place yourself consistently below the middle or above the middle of the scale? Did you place your "popular" examples more often above or below the middle? Is your place on each scale more like, or more in contrast to, that of those who seek popularity in the world?

Popularity's Price

Invite your players to perform the power play. Then distribute student page 2. Direct the students into groups of three or four to share their responses to the questions.

After discussing the questions, ask the students why it's so tempting at times to sacrifice morals and values for the sake of popularity. (There are many different reasons. Most of the reasons, however, come down to the simple fact that no one wants to be excluded. Satan often uses this great desire for belonging to lure us into disobedience to God's Word.)

Read aloud Romans 5:18 as a proclamation of how we became popular once again with our heavenly Father through the death of Jesus Christ.

Consequently, just as the result of one trespass was condemnation for all men, so also the result of one act of righteousness was justification that brings life for all men. For just as through the disobedience of the one man the many were made sinners, so also through the obedience of the one man the many will be made righteous. (Romans 5:18–19)

Remind students that Jesus became unpopular in order that we might receive forgiveness for the times we have compromised our values and principles for the sake of popularity. Jesus' life, death, and resurrection brings us back into favor with God whom we've disobeyed. Lead the students in prayer, asking forgiveness for the times they've sinned in seeking popularity, and giving thanks to God for His forgiveness and help in being obedient to God's Word in all areas of life, including the area of popularity.

Get Real!

Distribute copies of student page 3. (For nicer copies, cover the student page information at the bottom and use colored or "parchment" paper.) Allow volunteers to share their reactions to the statement. Do they agree? Disagree? What is an example of this in their lives or the lives of those they know? Invite the students to take this page home and post it somewhere in their rooms.

Closing

Close with a prayer. Give thanks for Christ's willingness to be sacrificed on our behalf and request His power as students are tempted to become popular with their friends through actions that are unpopular with God.

Popularity's Price

Circle all that apply. Be prepared to discuss why you chose that particular response.

1. Pamela Party
   - is my kind of girl.
   - is headed for trouble.
   - is like many kids I know.
   - _____.

2. Freida Foulmouth
   - is sort of like me.
   - is like my grandmother.
   - listens to cool music.
   - _____.

3. Carl Cool
   - is my kind of guy.
   - is like my best friend.
   - leaves me "cold."
   - _____.

4. Review these statements by Carl. To what degree is the statement correct? incorrect?
   - "Come on, nobody ever gets caught."
   - "Everybody does it."

5. Agree or disagree.
   - "Popularity is a form of success that's seldom worth the things we have to do in order to affirm it."
   - "When a person sells principles for popularity, he or she is soon bankrupt."

© 1995 CPH

Power Plays 2, Student Page 2

Get Real

Ask yourself: Which is more real? The "new creation" God creates in you through the Spirit of Christ, or the popular images to which we sometimes aspire? When we compete for popularity according to the standards of the world, we move down to its level. When, by God's grace, we speak up for and affirm His values as our own, we invite others to rise to those standards. If we move with the crowd, we'll stay with the crowd. A dumb idea, widely held and popular, is still a dumb idea. Swimming with the tide takes us only in the tide's direction.

If you believe in something that's true, noble, right, pure, lovely, admirable, excellent, or praiseworthy [Philippians 4:8], stand up for it with the power God gives. It may be that others will get smart and drift your way.

Power Play 2

Popularity's Price

(Four copies of this script are needed.)

But you are a chosen people, a royal priesthood, a holy nation, a people belonging to God, that you may declare the praises of Him who called you out of darkness into His wonderful light. Once you were not a people, but now you are the people of God; once you had not received mercy, but now you have received mercy. (1 Peter 2:9–10)

Characters

- REPORTER—a writer for "Me" magazine
- PAMELA PARTY—a gum-chewing "Miss Popularity" contest winner
- FREIDA FOULMOUTH—a popular student in school
- CARL COOL—a popular kid wearing dark sunglasses

Props (Optional)

- Four chairs
- Note pad and pencil for REPORTER
- Bubble gum
- Dark sunglasses

REPORTER: Pamela, Freida, Carl, thank you so much for giving me some of your precious time for this interview for *Me* magazine. As you know, *Me* magazine addresses itself to those who have gone beyond other popular magazines. First we were interested in *People,* then we wanted to read about *Us.* Now we have a magazine that talks about what's really important in life—*me!* And today, from everything I've heard, I've found three people who know a lot about *me. (She laughs toward the others.)* Oh, I don't really mean "me," I mean about yourselves. I'd like each of you to tell the readers of *Me* how you became so popular. Our *Me* readers want to know how they can become popular like you—or at least dream about it. That's what *Me* magazine is all about!

PAMELA PARTY: Me-oh-my, thank you for asking me. You're right, I do like talking about me! And *I* have lots to say about *myself.*

REPORTER: Most recently, Pamela, you were elected Miss Popularity of Mount Mississippi High School. Tell me how you became the most popular girl in high school.

PAMELA PARTY: Me-oh-my! *(She giggles.)* It's because I'm no stick-in-the-mud. Life is one big party, and I'm queen of the parties. That's why I make people call me "Pamela Party." As I see it, I'll only go around once in life, so why not enjoy it?

REPORTER: Very interesting, Pamela. Did you aspire all your life to become so popular?

PAMELA PARTY: Yeah, all my life. I wanted to be accepted. I wanted approval. I wanted to be included. I wanted to be invited. I wanted to be wanted. And so I set out to do just that.

REPORTER: What price did you have to pay for such approval, such inclusion, for the invites, to be wanted?

PAMELA PARTY: It required … well … it required everything!

REPORTER: So popularity was—and still is—pretty expensive?

PAMELA PARTY: You might say so.

REPORTER: How expensive?

PAMELA PARTY: Well … it required some compromise on my part … my grades … my parents' approval … my morals at times … but don't get me wrong—it was worth it!

18

REPORTER: Thank you, Miss Party. What about you, Freida Foulmouth? Everyone in your school says you fit right in. What is it exactly that makes you so popular?

FREIDA FOULMOUTH: Well, I speak everyone's language. Even the guys say I speak like one of them.

REPORTER: Does your last name tell us anything about what kind of language you use?

FREIDA FOULMOUTH: Yeah, I guess some people might call my language foul, but it isn't! It's very much in tune with the rap music we all listen to. It's a language that says a lot about how we feel!

REPORTER: Let me see if I understand. Using the language you do makes you popular?

FREIDA FOULMOUTH: You'd better believe it! It makes me part of them and them a part of me … if you get what I mean.

REPORTER: I think so! Our last person from our panel of experts on popularity is Carl Cool. As we interviewed student after student in Carson High School, asking who the most popular kid was, Carl's name was mentioned over and over again. Carl, just why are you so popular?

CARL COOL: I'm a leader, you know? I'm always up on what the right people think or wear or do—and that's what I do! I know and do what's cool.

REPORTER: What do you mean by "cool"?

CARL COOL: Hey, if ya gotta' ask … you're not, okay? I live by some awesome basic principles.

REPORTER: Like what?

CARL COOL: Like, "Come on, nobody ever gets caught"; and "Everybody does it."

REPORTER: Hmmm. I'm going to throw out a few quotations on popularity, and I'm wondering if you three popular kids would tell me if you agree or disagree. Okay, the first quote is:

"Popularity is a form of success that's seldom worth the things we have to do in order to attain it."

FRIEDA FOULMOUTH: Who said such a stupid thing! If you wouldn't be quoting me, I'd tell you what I thought of that statement.

REPORTER: Thank you, Miss Foulmouth. We're grateful you're refraining.

CARL COOL: For me, success is popularity … and popularity is … uh … like, you know … success!

REPORTER: That's very profound, Carl! What about this statement: "When a person sells principles for popularity, he or she is soon bankrupt."

PAMELA PARTY: The statement should read, "If a person doesn't sell his or her principles for popularity, he or she will always be bankrupt."

REPORTER: I see. How about this final statement: "The most popular person on earth is still Jesus. More people know about Him than any other person, even though He lived on this earth hundreds of years ago."

FRIEDA FOULMOUTH *(as if complimenting herself):* I use Jesus' name all the time. He even gets mentioned in some of our rap songs.

PAMELA PARTY: Jesus? If He was the most popular person on the earth, why was He crucified? Doesn't say much for Him, does it?

CARL COOL: I can do without *that* kind of popularity.

REPORTER: Well, thank you! I'm sure *Me* readers will become wiser about how to become more popular as they read the advice you've all shared with us today. I hope that we'll be able to interview you again, maybe 10 years from now, and see how popular you are then.

PAMELA PARTY: I'm sure I speak for all of us. It was fun. Thank you for caring about what's most important in life—me!

3

When Friends Make Me Choose

Focus

Young people place high value on friendship, and friends exert a strong influence in each young person's life. Our human nature and the work of Satan make it likely that earthly friendships may disappoint us or diminish our ability to live as faithful children of God. Jesus proved His love and friendship by fulfilling these words and dying for us. Even when we hurt Him, He still gathers us to Him and calls us "friend."

Objectives

By the power of Christ at work through His Word and Spirit the students will

1. recognize the impact—both good and bad—that their friendships can have on their lives;
2. give thanks for the perfect friendship that God has provided in our Savior, Jesus Christ;
3. rely on God's Word and Spirit to guide their choices of and relationships with friends.

A Powerful Word for the Leader

For additional perspective on this topic a devotional study is available for the leader. It is "Divided Loyalties between Friends," unit 2, study 3, found in *Power Words: Devotional Studies for Youth Bible Study Leaders*, CPH 20-2629.

This Study at a Glance

Activity	Time	Materials
Listen Up!	10 minutes	
Caught in the Middle	10 minutes	Copies of student page 4
From My Point of View	15 minutes	Three copies of power play 3, copies of student page 5
Into the Word	15 minutes	Bibles
Closing	5 minutes	

Listen Up!

Number your students 1 or 2 alternately around the table or room. Explain that you will select one person to be a treasure hunter. You will designate a "treasure" (a person, object, or place in the classroom) to the class without revealing it to the treasure hunter. One half of the class will seek to guide the treasure hunter to the treasure with correct verbal instructions, and one half will try to mislead the treasure hunter with false information. You will designate one group—either the 1's or 2's—to give false information, again without the treasure hunter's knowledge. (An easy way to do this is to send the hunter out of the room while you designate the treasure and the misleading group. You may be able to do this just by having the treasure hunter close his or her eyes while you point out the treasure and hold up one or two fingers for the class to see.)

Allow the volunteer about two minutes to find the person, object, or place that is it with the help of both groups of students. You can make this exercise more difficult by switching groups (again in a way that the volunteer can not see) in the middle of the exercise so that the misleading group starts giving correct instructions. When two minutes are up, or when the volunteer succeeds, choose a new volunteer. Play three or more games as time allows.

Then discuss the game. "How did it feel to be the volunteer? To whom did you listen? Why? Were the directions you followed the right ones?" Point out to the group that very often we receive different signals from people who say that they are our friends and we can become confused as to which direction we should take. The loudest and most persuasive voice isn't always the best voice.

Caught in the Middle

Divide into groups of three to five students. Give each group two copies of student page 4. Appoint one or more persons in each group to argue "let's do it" and one or two to be opposed. Appoint the last one in the group to represent the main character in the situation. Allow time for the students to roleplay their situation. Direct the main character to make a decision based on the influence of the others in his or her group. Discuss the decisions made in each group. Ask why each choice was made in a particular way. Whom was it hardest and easiest to listen to? Why?

From My Point of View

Say, "Making friends and keeping them can be one of the most difficult things in the world. Sometimes we choose friends for the wrong reasons. Sometimes our friends can lead us to make harmful choices. Let's see how that happens with Heather, Julie, and Alex." Let the play begin.

After the play is finished, invite comments. Distribute copies of student page 5 and direct the students to share their responses to questions 1–4 in small groups. You could use the groups from the previous exercise.

Explain, "It is obvious that choosing the right friends is not an easy task. There is also no doubt that we will be disappointed by some of the friendships we form during our lifetime." Ask the students to list some qualities of a good friend in the space on the student page. Invite volunteers to share responses. Write their suggestions on newsprint or on the board. Then say, "Someone once remarked, 'A friend is someone who knows all about you and loves you anyway.' This is the kind of friend we long for and hope to have. The good news is that we can have that friend for the rest of our lives."

Into the Word

For a brief Bible study, invite the students to open to Job 19:13–21. Explain that the book of Job tells the story of a man who, by Satan's evil plot and under God's watchful approval, lost his family, his possessions and wealth, and even his health. Job experienced all sorts of tragedy and turmoil in his life, yet he sought to keep alive his faith in God's promise and power. His friends, though, were quick to criticize and condemn him. In a dark moment, filled with despair, Job acknowledges his utter separation from everyone. Read, or have volunteers read, the section aloud.

Then ask:

> What are some words to describe Job's state of mind? (Alienated, estranged, forgotten, ridiculed.)
>
> What seems to be the saddest part of his confession? ("Those I love have turned against me.")
>
> Why is it so painful to be abandoned by a friend? (Answers will vary. It is the nature of friendship that we expect friends to be loyal and true.)
>
> Have you ever been "let down" by someone? (Allow a few volunteers to share if the group is comfortable with each other.)

Then ask students to recall (or to locate) John 3:16–17 in their Bibles. Read the verses aloud together from a common translation. Point out that Jesus loves us and wants to be our friend. When earthly friendships change and become unstable, He is there for us. When people disappoint us, He is still there. When everything around us seems hopeless, He is present with His comfort. God is always ready to pick us up when we fall, encourage us, and start us on the right path again. But He does even more.

God empowers people to be kind to each other and share His love. Remember Alex in our play. Even though snubbed and ignored, Alex felt compassion and sought to help. That is the measure of a true friend and real unselfish giving. That kind of love is the kind that our heavenly Father has for us.

Finally, look up John 15:9–17. Point out that fellowship with Jesus—living in Him like a branch connected to the vine—extends also to our relationships with others. As Christians we hear Jesus' command, "Love each other." He has made us His friends. In response we live with parents or neighbors or classmates in peace and gentle respect—in friendship. In our walk with Christ, there is no room for stubborn pride or feelings of superiority. Jesus loves us, cares for us, and sticks by us as a best friend. With such a friend as our Savior and Lord, we are able to relate to all people with His perfect love.

For an illustration of true friendship, direct students to the story of David and Jonathan (1 Samuel 18:1–4; 20:1–42).

Closing

Read or have the students read Psalm 139:1–4, 23–24. Close with a prayer like this:

Oh, Lord, You know us better than we know ourselves. Help us to know that You are truly our dearest friend. Bless us with friends who also know and trust in You. Work in our lives through Your Word and Spirit so that we may both have and be good friends. Lord, help us to encourage each other, accept each other, and be real friends to each other. In Your name we pray this. Amen.

Caught in the Middle

1. You and your two friends are alone in the house. There is going to be a party at your house; there are several cases of beer and soda in ice chests ready for the party. Your mom has said you and your friends could each have a soda. It's a hot day. You are all very thirsty. As you choose your sodas, one of your friends pulls out and opens a can of beer "by mistake," and then suggests that you each have one. Who will ever know? The other friend tells you it is wrong.

2. You are in charge of your little brother. You've decided to take him to a movie and have invited some of your friends along. There is an R-rated film playing at the same time in an adjoining theater. One friend suggests that you send your brother in to watch his movie while the rest of you catch the more "mature" show. Others say it isn't a good idea.

3. You arrive at a youth meeting with your friends only to find a sign on the door that says the youth leader is ill and the evening has been cancelled. One of your friends wants to head for the mall until the regular meeting would be over. If you call your parents first, you know you will have to go home. Others think you should call for permission anyway.

From My Point of View

1. Heather made the statement, "At least they say they're my friends." What do you think she meant?

2. Julie's comment was, "I could hardly wait till [Heather] introduced me to some of the guys I really liked." What kind of friend was she looking for?

Complete the following statement:

" A good friend is like a …"

3. Alex said, "[I know] something is really wrong, but she won't talk about it." What do you think Alex should do?

4. Of the three, which one would you want most for your own friend and why?

© 1995 CPH

Power Plays 2, Student Page 5

Power Play 3: From My Point of View

(Three copies of this script are needed.)

Whatever is true, whatever is noble, whatever is right, whatever is pure, whatever is lovely, whatever is admirable—if anything is excellent or praiseworthy—think about such things. Whatever you have learned or received or heard from me, or seen in me—put it into practice. And the God of peace will be with you. (Philippians 5:8–9)

Summary

We sometimes make the wrong choices in choosing friends. Sometimes our friendships place us in positions where we have to make hard choices. Our best friends are friends with whom we share common values and a common faith. Only one of these three people stays focused on what is right and good—even though it means rejection.

Characters

- HEATHER—a popular party girl
- JULIE—an outsider
- ALEX—Julie's equally out-of-it friend (could be a boy or girl)

HEATHER: It started out as a lark, you know? I never thought it would go this far. I mean, we were just going to have fun. The kids dared me to do it. In our circle, you always take a dare. It's just the way things are. I guess I should tell you something about myself, shouldn't I? I've always been pretty, and I've always had plenty of money for anything I wanted. I've been a cheerleader since eighth grade, and I can pretty much choose which boys I want to date. I make fairly good grades in school—that's pretty easy too. And I have a really big group of friends—at least they say they're my friends. I never thought much about what real friendship is until I met Julie. She was one of those nerdy-type people, you know? They don't dress quite right, and they are always hanging at the edge of the crowd. Julie would always sit at lunch by herself or with this one friend she had. She'd watch us when she thought we weren't looking. I could see it in her eyes, that longing to be one of us. It gave me kind of a superior feeling, because I knew she envied me. Then one day someone dared me to make friends with her, just to see what she would do. I said that was a stupid idea, but they kept on daring me. So I thought, why not, it might be good for a laugh. At first she didn't believe that I wanted to be her friend. I think that was the challenge, to make her believe I really liked her. So I began hanging out with her while my friends watched and laughed. I was really surprised when I discovered that she liked a lot of the things I liked and that she was really sensitive and understanding. I found myself telling her things I hadn't ever told anyone, and I began to value her friendship. I had never had a friend who cared like she did, or who would really listen to me and understand me. My other friends began to tease me for spending so much time with her. I couldn't tell them I really liked her. I knew they would laugh at me, and I would lose them as friends. I just couldn't sacrifice my popularity and all my friends—I just couldn't!

JULIE: I couldn't believe it! *She* really wanted to be my friend. All through school I had admired her. She was so pretty and she always had people around her. She was as *popular* as I was *un*popular. I used to dream that I was Heather and that I had all of her wonderful clothes and gorgeous hair. My grandparents had raised me since I was two years old. Grandma loved me a lot, but she was in her sixties and her ideas for dressing and hair styles were not exactly current. She was so strict! I wasn't even allowed to wear lipstick yet, even though I was 16. I didn't fit in at school. Alex was my only friend. And now, all of a sudden, there was Heather. She was standing there, asking me to come over to her house. I couldn't believe she was really talking to me. She must have known I couldn't believe it, because she looked at me kind of funny and then told me that she wouldn't have asked me to come over if she hadn't been serious. She smiled one of her dazzling smiles, and I stammered something like, "Sure I'll come." I totally forgot about Alex, who was sitting next to me. Nothing could have stopped me from going to Heather's. If anyone could help me to be popular and accepted, she could. So I went. Her house was just as beautiful as I knew it would be. Thick carpets and huge rooms. Heather's room was on the second floor, and she had a window seat that looked out over the park. We sat and talked for a long time on that first day. I was surprised to find out how much we had in common, and gradually I began to feel as though I was really valuable. I felt like she really cared about my opinion and how I felt inside. It was terrific. I began going places with her, and she even sat beside me in some of my classes. I could hardly wait till she introduced me to some of the guys I really liked. I knew they would go out with me if she just said the word. Then she told me about this party that was coming up. I knew my grandmother wouldn't approve. It wasn't going to be chaperoned, and there would be drinking. Alex said I was getting in over my head, but I really didn't listen. It's my life, I said. The choice was mine to make. Anyway, I lied to my grandmother and went to the party. I didn't plan on drinking anything, but they kept asking me to try it, and I had to choose. I knew one drink wouldn't hurt anything. I discovered that warm "buzz" inside made me feel more comfortable and accepted. I really liked that feeling. When Heather told me our friendship was over, to stop hanging around her, I couldn't believe it. What had I done wrong? I was so miserable. Then I remembered the alcohol at the party and how good it made me feel. I began to sneak some from my grandfather's liquor cabinet, just a little, and then more and more. Now I drink a lot, and lie a lot. I don't feel warm and comfortable when I drink anymore, but I can't stop.

ALEX: Julie is my friend. I've known her for as long as I can remember. I could never get her to go to youth group. She said that a lot of people she saw at church had no business being there—that they only acted like Christians. I tried to tell her that Christians aren't perfect, but she was always so stubborn. I was there the day that Heather came up and asked to be her friend. I was really suspicious. I had seen Heather talking to her friends just before she came over, and I was sure there was more to it than her really wanting to be Julie's friend. She invited Julie to her house, and I heard Julie accept. I tried to tell Julie she was making a big mistake. She became angry and told me that I was just jealous because Heather hadn't invited me to come along too. She said I had no right to make her choose between friends. I told her at least to be careful. She said that if I wanted to be her friend, I should keep my mouth shut. I didn't see Julie for weeks! She was with Heather and her group almost constantly. She and Heather seemed to be the best of friends. Julie was always at Heather's beck and call. It made me angry to see how Heather's friends laughed behind Julie's back, but she just didn't seem to notice. There was going to be a really big party at Shawn's house one weekend. No parents, but lots of booze. News like that gets around pretty fast at school. Somehow I felt that I just had to try one more time to warn Julie about what she was getting into. She laughed at me and said that I was a prude and should mind my own business. She told me she was capable of making choices on her own. She wasn't going to drink, anyway. When I asked her what she was going to tell her grandmother, she looked a little guilty. Then she kind of smiled and said that it would be really easy. She would tell her that she was going to a slumber party at Heather's. I tried to talk her out of going, but she turned her back on me and left. After the party something happened to Julie. She stopped hanging around with Heather. Now she spends all of her time alone, and she won't even talk to me. Something is really wrong, but she won't talk about it. Maybe, someday she'll let me help her. I keep praying about it, anyway.

What Will I Do with My Life?

This Study at a Glance		
Activity	Time	Materials
Getting Going	10 minutes	
Dialog with God	7 minutes	Two copies of power play 4
Into the Word	15 minutes	Bibles
God's Word at Work	15 minutes	Student page 6
*Living It	10 minutes	Index card and a pencil or pen for each person
Closing	3 minutes	

Advance preparation or special supplies required.

Getting Going

Ask, "How many times do you suppose you have been asked about what you want to be when you grow up? Think back to when you were about five years old, in kindergarten, or 1st grade. Let's list some of those jobs and occupations with which we've answered that question." Make a list on the board or newsprint.

"Let's move along in time to just a few years ago, to when you were in middle school or junior high school. What did you want to do when you were 11 or 12 years old?" Make a list of these ideas in a column next to the previous list.

Dialog with God

How about today? We will get to your responses in a minute, but first let's look at Maria, a 17-year-old high school junior, as she considers the same question, "What do you want to be when you grow up?" Maria walks up and the play begins. After the play, ask the following questions:

1. Have you ever felt like Maria? What was the situation like for you? (Accept all answers.)
2. Why do you think some parents act like Maria's parents? (Accept all answers.)

Focus

Eternal life is a free gift from God through the suffering, death, and resurrection of Jesus Christ. Our life here on earth as God's people is also a gift. God is at work in us through the power of His Word so that the many decisions we make about our lives and the future will serve Him.

Objectives

By the power of Christ at work through His Word and Spirit the students will

1. share ideas of what they think God is calling them to do with their life;
2. see the role that God has in their life as they make decisions about the future;
3. write a statement of purpose for their life as they live in God's hands.

A Powerful Word for the Leader

For additional perspective on this topic a devotional study is available for the leader. It is "Career Decisions," unit 2, study 4, found in *Power Words: Devotional Studies for Youth Bible Study Leaders*, CPH 20-2629.

3. What would you like from your parents as you make career plans and life decisions? (Answers will vary.)

4. Do you think God has a specific purpose and an exact plan for everyone's life? (Accept all answers. While God has some specific purposes for us as His people, it is not likely that God has predetermined every result in our lives or that He dictates the path we take. Refer back to the play and God's imaginary conversation with Maria.)

5. What is the difference between the two—purpose and plans? (Purpose has to do with end results; plans are the steps along the way.)

Into the Word

Read or have volunteers read Joshua 1:1–11. Then ask, "What are the plans and purpose that God has for Joshua?" (God intends for Joshua, as Moses' successor, to lead Israel across the Jordan River into the Promised Land. He has been preparing Joshua for this task by developing him as a righteous man and by giving him and supporting him in minor leadership roles. For instance, Joshua was an "aide to Moses" [Exodus 24:13] and one of the spies who entered Canaan [Numbers 13].) "What promise did God give Joshua that He still promises us today?" (v. 5 and v. 9: "I will be with you." See also Matthew 28:20.) "In what specific ways is God present with us as we live out His plans and purpose for our lives?" (He is present through His Word as we worship and study, in the Christian counsel of friends and elders, in the authorities He places over us, and through His influence on the events that occur in our lives.)

God's Word at Work

Distribute copies of the student page and ask the students to fill out the grid listing "Things I'd Like to Do," "Reasons Why," and "The Benefit for Me and Others."

After students have had sufficient time to do this, ask for a few volunteers to share their work. Then continue the activity with the following questions. (In each case the answers are matters of opinion. Affirm especially those responses that are informed by the previous discussion and the application of God's Word.)

1. Are there any patterns that are present in your grid (such as money, power, fame, or popularity)?

2. Why do people work (other than for the money)?

3. Which of our responses are obviously Christian? Which ones are not?

4. How will you know which of the things you've listed you should do?

5. Can you do a job that is not outwardly Christian and remain steadfast as a believer? Are there some types of jobs or careers that Christians should not enter?

6. Look at your favorite response. As God is "with you" in the future, just as He was with Joshua, how might you serve His purposes?

Living It

It has become very popular in our time to see corporations and businesses publish and display what is called a mission statement.

A mission statement is a communication of the unique reason or purpose a company has for existing. A mission statement is the beginning point for a company as its leaders develop their strategic plan for business. Recently, some writers have stressed the importance for individuals to have a personal mission statement.

A personal mission statement is a statement of an individual's unique reason or purpose for the existence of their life. Here are two examples.

> A Christian college professor—"I am committed to enhancing desire and skills, in individuals and groups, for more effective service to church and community through creative educational processes."
>
> A parish DCE—"My goal in life is to study God's Word constantly so that I may grow in my faith and in my ability to discern His will, to live my life to God's glory, to love and work for Him, and to serve and encourage my family in the love and fear of God."

Distribute index cards and invite each student to write a rough draft of a personal mission statement that will reflect his or her unique reason or purpose in the life that God has given him or her to live. If time allows, let volunteers share their statements.

Closing

Close with a prayer that God may continue to be with those present, that they may be strong and courageous, and that they may discover the purposes that God has for them in life.

What Will I Do with My Life?

Directions: In each section fill in as many of the jobs, careers, and life experiences that you can think of that you would like to have over the course of your life.

Things I'd Like to Do	Reasons Why	The Benefit for Me and Others

© 1995 CPH

Power Plays 2, Student Page 6

Power Play 4

Dialog with God

(Two copies of this script are needed.)

No one will be able to stand up against you all the days of your life. As I was with Moses, so I will be with you; I will never leave you nor forsake you. Be strong and courageous, because you will lead these people to inherit the land I swore to their forefathers to give them. Be strong and very courageous. Be careful to obey all the law my servant Moses gave you; do not turn from it to the right or to the left, that you may be successful wherever you go. (Joshua 1:5–7)

Theme

God has plans for us, but sometimes it is only through patient prayer and reflection that we know His will for our lives.

Characters

- MARIA—17-year-old high school student
- GOD—a voice that is heard offstage

MARIA: I am so frustrated! No, I'm mad! Really mad! They just don't understand! Oh, God, what am I going to do?

GOD: Whatever you want.

MARIA: What? Who is that? Who's there?

GOD: It's Me; you called Me, didn't you?

MARIA: Scott, is that you? Little brother, where are you? Who is this really?

GOD: I'm not your little brother; I'm your *heavenly* Father.

MARIA: What? I can't believe this!

GOD: It's true. I'm here to listen to you. Sounds like you have a problem.

MARIA: Oh, wow! You really *are* God!

GOD: Always have been; always will be.

MARIA: And, yes, I do have a problem. A confusing one.

GOD: I know.

MARIA: It's my parents; they just don't understand! It's my life! They have their own ideas about what I should do.

GOD: And that is?

MARIA: They want me to be a teacher. Mom was a teacher. Grandma was a teacher in a one-room schoolhouse. They say it's a good job. It's something that you can do for many years. You can go back to it after a family is grown. You can do it part-time. You can even do private tutoring. It makes sense to them.

GOD: But it doesn't make sense to you.

MARIA: No, it doesn't, because I don't want to teach. I don't want to be in a classroom all day. I don't want to grade papers. I don't want to make cute bulletin boards. That's just not me.

GOD: What is you?

MARIA: I don't know—that's what makes it so frustrating. I just don't know. My parents want me to know, soon. I'm only a junior in high school so I think I have time. But my parents say I need to make plans to go to college soon, so I need to apply to the right schools. I need to know what I want to study, and I need to take the SAT or the ACT or one of those tests! But I can't decide! Hey, wait a minute—you're God; you know everything. You tell me what I'm supposed to do.

GOD: Do whatever you want to do!

MARIA: What? What kind of answer is that? Aren't you supposed to have a plan for my life?

GOD: I do.

MARIA: Then tell me what it is.

GOD: I sent My Son, Jesus, to earth. He came and walked and lived among the people. He made friends. Jesus told them about Me and how much I love them and how I was going to save them from their sins and eternal punishment. For this plan to work My Son died. He died so that His friends and all people might live forever. He died, Maria, so that you would be free—now and forever. Free from sin, death, and the power of the devil. Free to live a life that responds to the love that My Son and I have for you.

MARIA: I don't feel so free.

GOD: But you are.

MARIA: I still don't understand.

GOD: You are free to make choices. Choices like what you want to do for a career. What job you want.

MARIA: You mean you don't have anything specific in mind?

GOD: No, I don't. I do have some thoughts on how you should live.

MARIA: Like what?

GOD: Like love Me, love others. Tell others about Me. Serve others in My Son's name.

MARIA: But, nothing like wanting me to be a teacher, or a doctor, or something like that?

GOD: If you wanted to be a teacher and it would serve others and bring you joy, I would be with you. If you wanted to be a doctor and it would serve others and bring you joy, I'd be there too.

MARIA: Is there anything you don't want me to be?

GOD: Maria, I think you are smart enough to answer that.

MARIA: Yeah, you're right.

Scripture quotations: NIV®
© 1995 CPH

GOD: Most of all, I don't want you to be unhappy. If teaching, as important as it may be, takes away the joy My Son has given you, then I wouldn't want you to be a teacher.

MARIA: Really! Can you tell my parents that? I know they'd listen to you!

GOD: I think I'll let *you* do that.

MARIA: What? Tell them I had a talk with you and that I felt you didn't want me to teach.

GOD: Sure.

MARIA: They'd think I was crazy.

GOD: It's the truth, isn't it?

MARIA: Yeah, that's true. You're pretty big on that truth stuff, aren't you?

GOD: Yes I am.

MARIA: This is a good talk we're having, but I still don't know what I should do.

GOD: What do you really want to do?

MARIA: No one's ever asked me that before. I guess … I guess … I'd like to do something with photography. I like to take pictures. Some of them are here on my wall.

GOD: I've noticed.

MARIA: I think I do okay, but I need more practice, and there is a lot more I want to learn.

GOD: So, go and learn it. Give it a try.

MARIA: Really? That's okay with You?

GOD: I'm with you, if that is your choice. And I'll support you even if you change your mind and decide to do something else.

MARIA: Really? That's great!

GOD: I'm always here to help.

MARIA: I guess I know that. I'll just have to talk about things like this with you more often.

GOD: Please do. I always enjoy hearing from you.

How Will I Know When I've Got It Made?

This Study at a Glance

Activity	Time	Materials
*How Do You Measure Up?	5 minutes	Measuring devices of various kinds
Exploring God's Word	15 minutes	Bible, pencils, copies of student page 7
*God's Word at Work!	20 minutes	Enlarged copies of student page 8 (Success!), play money, nickels and pennies, dice or other random number device (see activity)
Living It	10 minutes	
Quality Control	10 minutes	Four copies of power play 5

Requires advance preparation or special supplies.

How Do You Measure Up?

Bring to class various measuring devices and discuss their use. For example, ask, "If I wanted to measure how tall you are, what would I use?" (Measuring tape.) "If I wanted to measure how fast you can run?" (Stop watch.) "If I wanted to measure how much flour to use to make a cake?" (Measuring cup.)

Then ask, "But what would I use if I wanted to measure how successful you are? What are some criteria by which people measure success?" List answers on the board or on a large sheet of newsprint as students offer suggestions. Some ideas might include money, car, grades, number of friends, happiness, fame, or power.

"Does every successful person have all of these things? Does every successful person *want* all of these things?" Ask students to name people they consider successful. List them. Match two or three with the components of success already listed. Work to include one or two prominent religious figures.

Lead the class to the conclusion that *success* means different things to different people.

Focus

Success at any price is a dangerous philosophy. With that goal, those who fail are overcome by despair. There are no winners because there is always another prize to win, another goal to achieve, more to want. To such fruitless striving, God brings the good news that we have already won. He has paid the price for our success. Everything that really matters is ours already through His death on the cross. By the power of the Holy Spirit, we live in the certainty that our hope of heaven will become a reality. Our success is assured!

Objectives

By the power of Christ at work through His Word and Spirit the students will

1. define success in the light of God's Word and will;
2. find comfort in the success Christ has won for them and receive it thankfully;
3. live confidently, as Christ gives them strength, pursuing goals with eternal significance.

A Powerful Word for the Leader

For additional perspective on this topic a devotional study is available for the leader. It is "The Honor Roll," unit 2, study 5, found in *Power Words: Devotional Studies for Youth Bible Study Leaders,* CPH 20-2629.

Exploring God's Word

Write this definition of success on the board: Success is "turning out as you had hoped." Operating with that definition, direct the class to take a look at some people mentioned in Scripture and analyze them according to the student page correlating with this lesson. The class may work in small groups to complete this activity, then report back to share their conclusions with the whole class. Their conclusions as to the success or failure of each person will depend on what they listed as that person's goal.

Suggested symbols of success or failure might include a safety pin for Hannah, a coin for the rich young man, a pen for the 70 disciples, a cross for Jesus. Point out that these symbols by themselves could mean anything. They become important only in the light of what they represent in each case. It is the same with all "status symbols" used to represent success. Their value is in the judgment of the user.

God's Word at Work

Ask, "What about you? Do you consider yourself a success? How can you tell?"

Direct students into groups of two or three to play Success! Each group will need a copy of the game board (student page 8) and a random number device. Enlarge the student page when you copy it, if possible. If you don't have dice on hand, use six index cards, numbered one through six—one set for each group. At each turn a player draws one of the cards and moves that number of spaces. The cards are shuffled before each turn. In preparation, give each class member a nickel or a penny and distribute play money as follows: Each player should receive 10 one-dollar bills and 20 five-dollar bills. (It will help to prepare play money ahead of time and place it in envelopes to be given out in class. As an alternative, each group could keep a paper bank account with no money changing hands.) If two people play in each group, the "Bank" should be supplied with 10 one-dollar bills, 20 ten-dollar bills, and 20 one-thousand-dollar bills. Allow the groups to play the game about 10 minutes or until each group has a winner.

Discuss the game. Bring out these points. "In the end, what was the only thing that mattered? Spending an eternity with God in heaven is the ultimate success. If that is our hope, we will be successful—because achieving that goal does not depend on us. It is already paid for and is available for us. In the process of arriving at our destination, we may experience other successes (or failures). They are ways of keeping score in a challenging and complicated world. Keeping success in perspective helps us cope each step along the way." Refer your students to Luke 12:22–34 (especially verses 32–34). Point out that God in His love guarantees our eternal "success"—salvation—*and* provides for our daily successes as well.

Living It

Encourage students to write down three or four personal goals for success in their lives. Write the following evaluation questions on newsprint or the board for all to see.

- How/Where will I achieve it?
- What will it cost?
- What good will it do?
- How long will it last?
- How will it affect others?
- How important is it? (1 to 10)
- How is God included?
- How will it affect my faith in God?

Talk about the goals and dreams of your students and share your goals and dreams with them. Ask, "Is it wrong to experience material success? Think about Jesus' comments to the rich young man. When does being 'successful' become a problem?" (It becomes a problem when it interferes with our relationship with God or others.)

"Do you consider your parents to be successful? Why or why not? How do you feel about your status in the world? What steps will you need to take now in order to achieve your plans?" After allowing a few volunteers to share, pray together or silently for God's blessing on these endeavors.

Quality Control

Watch the play at this time as a summary of the lesson.

Pray, "We too shout yes in victory, oh, Lord, for You have given us everything worth having—especially eternal life with You. We praise Your name now and for all eternity. Amen."

Exploring God's Word

Name	Reference	Hope	Success/Failure	Symbol
Adam	Genesis 3	To be like God	F	Thorn
Hannah	1 Samuel 1–2			
Rich Man	Mark 10:17–31			
70 Disciples	Luke 10:1–20			
Jesus	(You choose)			

Success

Directions: Play with one, two, or three other players. One player serves as the "Bank." Each player selects a different coin to use as a marker and places it on step 1. Yes, a nickel is worth more than a penny, but that's life. Some people, through no doing of their own, seem to have an advantage right from the start. Roll the die and proceed around the route according to the number rolled. Collect or pay all money to "the bank" at each space. You must land on space 20 by an exact count to win.

You are born. Collect $10 from Aunt Martha. Happy birthday! 	Late in toilet training.  Pay $2 for extra diapers.	Lost first tooth.  Collect $1 from the tooth fairy.	Great report card. 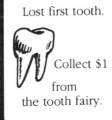 Collect $10 from Dad.	Christmas outfit needed.  Pay $10 to the mall.
Scholarship to college or university of your choice. Collect $2,000. 	SAT tutor.  Pay $30.	High school band/cheerleading uniform.  Pay $100.	Grade school graduation.  Collect $500 from assorted relatives.	Little League expenses.  Pay $10 for pizza.
Graduation party.  Pay $1 to caterer for each friend invited.	College degree. Collect $5,000. You made it!	Nose job. Pay $400.	Engagement ring. Pay (if boy) $300. Collect (if girl) $300.	Wedding of the century.  Pay $5,000.
Death. To reach heaven pay $777,777. Get into heaven free if you know the "manager"— just say, "Jesus sent me." CONGRATULATIONS! YOU WIN!	Collect Social Security payment of $5.	Give regularly to church. Put whatever percentage you feel like in the offering plate.	High-paying job.  Pay 50% of assets to IRS.	Birth of bright, attractive children. Pay doctor $30 per child.

Power Play 5
Quality Control

(Four copies of this script are needed.)

However, do not rejoice that the spirits submit to you, but rejoice that your names are written in heaven. (Luke 10:20)

Characters

- SHAWNA
- WILLY
- JILLIAN
- QUALITY CONTROL ANGEL

Setting

A waiting room. SHAWNA, WILLY, and JILLIAN sit side by side on a bench or on three chairs placed next to each other.

Props (Optional)

- Tarnished trophy
- Official-looking, wrinkled document
- Purse
- Clipboard
- Windshield-wiper blade
- Tape measure
- Three fairly large paper crosses

WILLY: What's keeping them so long? We've been waiting forever! *(He looks at watch.)* Hey, that's funny—no numbers.

JILLIAN: You don't *need* numbers on your watch any more, stupid. This is eternity! We *will* be waiting forever.

SHAWNA: I told you not to drive so fast. But, no-o-o! You had to try to beat the light.

WILLY: Look, I said I was sorry. Just chill, okay?

SHAWNA: It is chilly in here. *(She shudders.)* What could be taking so long? We're dead, right? What more could they be waiting for? Are we going to get "deader"?

JILLIAN: No, I think this is as dead as we get. This couldn't have happened at a worse time. Just when I got picked for the varsity team. What's going to happen to my letter jacket? I put down a deposit. My mother'll kill me if … Oh, I guess it's too late for that now.

WILLY: At least we've got a chance. Heaven is for good people, right? All we have to do is prove that we're successful and kind to animals and stuff, and they've *got* to let us in.

JILLIAN: I saw how you treated your little sister. You could be in big trouble.

SHAWNA: I don't know, it's kind of hard to measure how good or successful you've been. What have you got to show for it?

WILLY: Fortunately, I had this with me in the car. *(He holds up trophy.)* I just picked it up from having it engraved. MVP, it says—Most Valuable Player. If that doesn't convince them, nothing will.

JILLIAN *(looking in her purse):* I think I've got my honor roll certificate in here some place. Yes, here it is. *(She pulls out a slightly wrinkled document.)* It's signed by Mr. Hanson himself—the principal. Do you think they've ever heard of him up here?

WILLY: I wouldn't count on it.

JILLIAN: I got three A's and two B's. That's pretty good for never cracking a book. Thank God for my photographic memory!

WILLY: And for Becky Wynn's homework that you copied.

SHAWNA: Boy, I really *am* in trouble. I don't have anything to show them.

JILLIAN: Haven't you ever won any prizes or awards?

38

SHAWNA: Not that I can think of.

WILLY: How about your driver's license? You passed the test for that, didn't you?

SHAWNA: Somehow, under the circumstances, I don't think anything that has to do with *driving* is going to impress them.

JILLIAN: What could be taking so long?

WILLY: Quiet! Here they come!

QUALITY CONTROL ANGEL *(walks onstage carrying clipboard):* Ah, there you are. Sorry to keep you waiting. We're really busy tonight. I am in charge of quality control. It is my job to determine whether or not you are successful enough to join the others inside.

JILLIAN: You *are* going to let us in, aren't you?

ANGEL: Well, let's see … *(He checks clipboard.)*

WILLY *(stands):* Look, I brought this trophy. It says I am—*was*—the most valuable player. I worked hard for it. The girls I knew were really impressed at the pep rally when it was presented. I was hoping to make all-conference this year. I …

ANGEL: This is heaven, son. We don't need any trophies here. Everybody makes touchdowns. *(WILLY sits down dejectedly.)*

JILLIAN *(stands):* This is my honor roll certificate. I've been on the honor roll every semester since preschool! I've earned hundreds of dollars from my parents for getting good grades. I was going to get a scholarship to …

ANGEL: There are lots of smart people in heaven, sweetie. Actually, we don't have much use for knowing all the world capitals or conjugating verbs. *(JILLIAN sits down. ANGEL looks at SHAWNA.)* How about you? Did you bring anything to show how successful you are?

SHAWNA *(stands up, worried):* Well, actually, I must have left all that stuff at home. We did leave in a hurry, you know. I'm sure I could have thought of *some*thing. Oh, wait a minute, I did go to youth group every week and even church most of the time—no matter how boring it got. And I washed the most windows at the last car wash! *(She pulls wiper blade out of her pocket.)* Here, I had this left over.

ANGEL: Sorry. Automobile parts belong—elsewhere! *(SHAWNA sits down. ANGEL looks at all three.)* I thought you all said you were successful.

WILLY: Sir, we thought we were doing our best down on earth. Everyone told us we *were* the best. What more could we have done?

ANGEL: That's just the point. People on earth measure success differently than we do up here. *(ANGEL pulls out a tape measure.)*

SHAWNA: What's that?

ANGEL: This is my official success-o-meter. Let's see how you measure up. *(To SHAWNA)* Come on, you first.

(SHAWNA stands. ANGEL holds tape measure up to her—head to toe.)

ANGEL: Just as I suspected. You'll have to scrunch down a little. Farther, farther … *(She does so until she is on her knees.)* There, now you are just right!

WILLY: Oh, I get it. Me too. *(He kneels.)*

JILLIAN: And me! *(She kneels too.)*

ANGEL: God is not impressed with trophies or awards—or windshield wipers! On your knees you demonstrate a humble heart that looks to Jesus for all you need. Will you trade your trophies for what He has instead? *(WILLY exchanges his trophy for a cross.)* Most Valuable Player? He has made you a Most Valuable Person, purchased with nothing less than His holy precious blood. *(JILLIAN exchanges her honor roll certificate for a cross.)* Honor roll? All honor and glory and wisdom are His. If you know Him, you have everything worth knowing. *(SHAWNA exchanges her windshield-wiper blade for a cross.)* Your car wash souvenir? He has washed *you* clean from all that would keep you out of heaven. You qualify at last! His success is yours, and you are His, forever! Welcome.

WILLY, SHAWNA, JILLIAN *(smile, raise arms in victory):* Yes!

Special People Special Purpose

Focus

We live in a sex-saturated society. Temptation is fierce, especially for young adults. We often fail to live up to God's standards for sexual purity in our thoughts, words, and actions. But God has forgiven us through Christ and has given us a special purpose and identity. Through the Holy Spirit God gives us strength to stand firm in the face of temptation and remain faithful.

Objectives

By the power of Christ at work through His Word and Spirit the students will

1. understand that they are God's chosen, holy people through Christ;
2. see some of the consequences of sexual impurity;
3. identify ways to avoid sexual temptation and stand firm in their faith.

A Powerful Word for the Leader

For additional perspective on this topic a devotional study is available for the leader. It is "In Sexuality—a Pig or a Bride?" unit 2, study 6, found in *Power Words: Devotional Studies for Youth Bible Study Leaders*, CPH 20-2629.

A Note for the Leader

Sexual sins are a difficult matter to overcome. Perhaps this is why Paul speaks so strongly about temptation in this area (1 Corinthians 6:15–20). God's law and instruction is for our protection and benefit, to spare

This Study at a Glance

Activity	Time	Materials
*It's All around Us	5 minutes	Newspapers and/or magazines
The "In" Crowd	10 minutes	Four copies of power play 6
Hot Time in Potiphar's House	5 minutes	Copies of student page 9
Who We Are	10 minutes	
A Note to Me	10 minutes	Copies of student page 9
The Connection	10 minutes	
Yeah, but What About …	5 minutes	
Closing	5 minutes	Blank paper

Requires advance preparation or special supplies.

It's All around Us

Hand out newspapers and/or magazines to your students. Have them go through and mark or cut out any ads that use sex appeal to sell a product. After a few minutes, ask the students to list the different ways advertisers use sex to influence consumers (you're sexy if you smoke this brand; drinking alcohol increases your attractiveness; sexy girls use this brand of hair color). Write the students' observations on the board. Then say, "We live in a sex-saturated society. It's all around us. And the pressure to conform to the world can be enormous. Let's look at how one couple withstood the pressure."

The "In" Crowd

Read aloud or watch the play. At the end of the play ask, "What do you think Mike and Beth will do? What would you do if you were them? What might be the result?

40

Hot Time in Potiphar's House

Hand out student page 9. Ask a volunteer to read aloud the story of Joseph and Potiphar's wife, Genesis 39:6–23. Then direct the students' attention to the first section of the student page. Ask them to answer the first two questions on their own. Read aloud the third question. Ask the students to read Genesis 39:9 and write their answers to the third question in the space provided on the student page. When all have finished, say, "Joseph refused Potiphar's wife because he knew that his actions would affect his relationship with Potiphar and with God. He understood the trust that both God and his master had placed in him. God gave Joseph strength for his decision so that he could be faithful to God and faithful to his calling.

us from the emotional and spiritual pain of sexual sin. In a society where such sin is treated casually and often encouraged, we need to point out the dangers of such a casual attitude. On the other hand, the Gospel reminds us of God's unconditional love and healing forgiveness. We need to make sure those who are under the weight of sexual sins hear the liberating message that Jesus has already paid for those sins.

Who We Are

Write on the board, "Hebrews 12:1–3" and "1 Peter 2:9." Below the references write, "Who We Are." Divide the class into groups of three or four. Ask the members of each group to look up one of the passages and describe in their own words their special identity or purpose. After a few minutes, ask the groups to share their discoveries. Write their comments under the "Who We Are" heading on newsprint or on the board. The following are some possible answers:

Hebrews 12:1–3—We are surrounded by other witnesses, other Christians; we are not to get entangled or hindered; there is a race marked out for us; we are called to focus on Jesus; He is our inspiration and example of faithfulness.

1 Peter 2:9—We are chosen by God; we are holy (set apart by God for a sacred purpose); we belong to God; our purpose is to declare God's praises (to tell what great things God has done in Christ and to show what a great God we have).

A Note to Me

Ask your students to think about the descriptions on the board. Remind them that these words provide a sure sense of identity and purpose for us as Christians. We are God's people, redeemed by the death of Jesus Christ, God's Son, given new life and strength through Him, and empowered to serve God in our daily lives. See Ephesians 1:4–12. (He chose us "for the praise of His glory"); 2 Corinthians 6:17–7:1 (God calls us to be holy out of reverence for Him); and Luke 1:68–74 (God has saved us to serve Him without fear).

Now ask, "If God were to write you a note reminding you to live according to His will and purpose, what would He write?" Ask the students to write their answers in the "A Note to Me" section of the student page. Encourage them to incorporate the descriptions on

Yeah, but What About ...

It may be that you will have students in your group who have gone too far sexually. They could be feeling extremely guilty. Raise the issue with your students by asking, "What about people, even Christians, who have gone too far or are in a sexually compromising relationship? Are they condemned? Have they totally blown it in God's eyes?" After a few minutes of discussion remind students of God's unconditional forgiveness. See Matthew 1:5 (Rahab the ex-prostitute mentioned in the geneology of Jesus); Jeremiah 31:3–4 (God's love is everlasting to the point of restoring us to "virgin" status in His eyes); Psalm 103:11–12 (God separates our sin from us as far as the east is from the west); and 1 John 1:9 (God will cleanse us from all unrighteousness).

Extending the Lesson

Let the students—individually, in small groups, or as a class—write an ending to the power play that illustrates how Mike and Beth respond to pressure from the "in" crowd. Challenge them to make it both realistic and positive.

---

the board. If the students are willing, ask a few volunteers to share their special notes from God.

The Connection

Remind your students that Joseph was able to resist sexual temptation because by God's grace he had a firm understanding of his place as God's child, what his purpose was, and the strength God provides. The passages from Hebrews and 1 Peter remind us that we, like Joseph, are God's children. We also have a special purpose. We are strengthened by God through Word and Spirit—through Bible study, worship, confession and forgiveness, and the Sacraments. The notes that the students wrote are reflective of a special identity and purpose.

Ask, "What do you think is the effect when all God's people ignore their purpose and identity as mentioned in Hebrews and 1 Peter?" (God's glory is not proclaimed; we go in any direction we want; we live wild lives.)

Say, "Sexual temptation—like all sin—threatens our relationship with God. What consequences might God's people suffer when giving in to sexual temptation? (Sexually transmitted diseases, guilt, rejection, unwanted pregnancies, diminished credibility in the world, hardness of heart, and damaged relationships with those who trust us such as parents and friends.)

Assure your students, "Just as God strengthened Joseph, so He will strengthen us. He enables us to 'fix our eyes on Jesus' (Hebrews 12:2) because He is the one that gives us a special and holy identity and purpose in our lives."

Closing

On blank paper or on the back of the student page, invite your students to write a brief prayer, thanking God for the special purpose and identity He has given them and asking for His strength to keep them faithful to that purpose. Invite volunteers to share their prayers. After a few moments of silent prayer say, "Dear God, we know that You have a special purpose for all of us. Thank You for your forgiveness when we fail to live up to that special purpose. We know that by faith, through the grace of the Holy Spirit, we will be empowered to resist all temptations that may lead us away from You. Amen."

Hot Time in Potiphar's House

1. What did Potiphar's wife want from Joseph?

   a. She wanted him to get an anchovy and pineapple pizza.

   b. She wanted change for a twenty.

   c. She needed help finding a contact lens.

   d. She wanted him to go to bed with her.

2. Why did he say no?

   a. He was weird.

   b. He had a headache.

   c. He didn't want to let God or his master down.

   d. She was ugly.

3. What do you think gave Joseph the strength to say no, even though it ended up getting him in trouble? (See Genesis 39:9.)

A Note to Me

Dear_____,

You are ...

Your special purpose is ...

God

© 1995 CPH

Power Play 6

The "In" Crowd

(At least four copies of this script are needed.)

Therefore, since we are surrounded by such a great cloud of witnesses, let us throw off everything that hinders and the sin that so easily entangles, and let us run with perseverance the race marked out for us. Let us fix our eyes on Jesus, the author and perfecter of our faith, who for the joy set before Him endured the cross, scorning its shame, and sat down at the right hand of the throne of God. Consider Him who endured such opposition from sinful men, so that you will not grow weary and lose heart. (Hebrews 12:1–3)

Summary

A young Christian couple is tempted by the "in" crowd to give up their special identities in Christ and join the "in" crowd and its worldly ways.

Characters

- MIKE—teenage boy
- BETH—teenage girl
- THE "IN" CROWD—Two to 10 teenage boys and girls, dressed as identically as possible. One of them is the LEADER.

Props (Optional)

- Hats or caps and sunglasses—a pair for everyone in the play.
- Large paper crosses with tape backing or on a yarn necklace—one for each player. Mike and Beth are already wearing theirs; the others should be available to THE "IN" CROWD, perhaps on the floor where they will line up onstage.

MIKE *(walks up to BETH and gives her a hug):* Hi Bethie, how are you?

BETH: Great! How was your math test?

MIKE: Incredible. I'm not sure how I did, though.

BETH: I'm sure you did fine; you studied pretty hard. I should know—I was there!

MIKE: Yep, you sure were. It seems that's all we do—study together. At your house. In the kitchen. With your parents and brother and sisters. Of course, sometimes we go completely crazy and study at *my* house. Boy, we really go nuts then.

BETH: I'm sensing a little sarcasm here.

MIKE *(sighs):* I'm sorry. I don't mean to take it out on you. It's just … Don't you feel like we're missing out on *something?*

BETH: Missing out on …

MIKE *(almost shouting):* Life! I was talking to some of the guys earlier, and they told me all about what they did with *their* girlfriends. Then they asked me if we had … you know … and I didn't know what to say. All we do is study or go to football or baseball games or go out with our friends from church or school. We don't do anything else.

BETH: I know what you mean. Girls talk too, you know. A lot of my friends' relationships have … advanced … a lot farther than ours has.

MIKE: Beth, I love you—

BETH: And I love you.

MIKE *(sighs again):* Sometimes I just wish we didn't care. Why not be like everyone else? They don't care, and they have such exciting lives!

BETH: Yeah, everyone in the "in" crowd does whatever they want! They don't care what anyone says about anything—and they're popular.

(THE "IN" CROWD *enters from stage left all wearing hats or caps, sunglasses in hand or pocket. They are all walking in formation; everything they do is identical. As they walk in, the leader snaps his fingers, and they all stop. He snaps again, and they all turn and face downstage. He snaps his fingers again, and they all take out sunglasses and put them on [Director—make up new things THE "IN" CROWD can do in sync!].)*

MIKE: They are *so* cool!

BETH: Wouldn't it be great to be like them?

(The leader of THE "IN" CROWD tips his glasses briefly and looks at MIKE and BETH.)

BETH: Hey! I think they noticed us!

MIKE: Quick, take out your sunglasses and act really cool!

(They cross stage left, put on sunglasses, and stand back to back just like THE "IN" CROWD. The leader sees them and motions to MIKE and BETH to join them.)

BETH: They noticed!

MIKE: Great! Let's join 'em.

(BETH and MIKE join THE "IN" CROWD in formation. The leader snaps his fingers, and they turn to the left and take two steps; he snaps his fingers again, and they stop; he snaps again, and they turn to face downstage.)

MIKE: I see a lot of my friends.

BETH *(excited)*: Me too.

MIKE: I can't believe we're *in* the "in" crowd.

(The LEADER of The "IN" CROWD snaps his fingers, and they take off their hats and toss them. The leader snaps again, and they pick up the crosses.)

MIKE: Cool—we already have these.

(The LEADER snaps his fingers, and they all turn to their right. He snaps again, and they take two steps. He snaps again, and they face downstage. He snaps again, and they take the crosses off and drop them. BETH pulls MIKE off to the side.)

BETH: Mike—we can't do that!

MIKE: Well, we wanted to be like them, didn't we? Everyone else took theirs off. Maybe we can take ours off for a little while and put them back on later.

BETH: Once we do, there's no turning back.

MIKE: The guys told me that it's easier the second time. Then after awhile, you really don't think about it—you just do it.

BETH: I don't know if I could "just do it."

(The leader walks to them and snaps his finger angrily. He points to all the crosses on the floor and then points at MIKE and BETH. The others stare at them, waiting. MIKE and BETH look at each other and the audience. The scene freezes and the play ends—for now.)

Who Values Life?

Focus

Life today is often considered valuable only for what it produces. Significance is attached to wealth, appearances, productivity, power, and influence. But in God's eyes each life is infinitely significant because He has created us in His own image and redeemed us through Jesus Christ.

Objectives

By the power of Christ at work in them through the Spirit the students will

1. thank God for the gift of life He has given them;
2. be able to explain that each life is precious to God and has value in His sight because all people are made in His image;
3. list activities they can do to help promote the sanctity of life.

A Powerful Word for the Leader

For additional perspective on this topic a devotional study is available for the leader. It is "The Value of a Life," unit 2, study 7, found in *Power Words: Devotional Studies for Youth Bible Study Leaders,* CPH 20-2629.

This Study at a Glance

Activity	Time	Materials
Decisions	10 minutes	Three copies of power play 7
*You Decide	15 minutes	Posters describing five people
In God's Image	10 minutes	Bible
*What's Your Approach?	10 minutes	Six-foot- to eight-foot-long two-by-four board or eight-foot string
Seeing the Value *or*	10 minutes	
What I Could Do	10 minutes	
Closing	5 minutes	

Advance preparation or special supplies required.

Decisions

Open by reading Psalm 139 aloud as a prayer. Introduce power play 7.

After the play is read, move into the study by saying something like, "One of the most controversial topics today is how we see life. Abortion, euthanasia, and assisted-suicide confront us with a number of issues. The question we want to answer is 'How should we, as Christians, respond?' "

You Decide

Write the following situations on sheets of paper. They should be large enough to be seen by the entire group when posted. Include the numbers for easy reference. Divide students into five pairs or small groups if possible. Post the situations and assign one to each small group, pair, or student. Direct the students to list the possible positive and negative impact their assigned individual might have on his or her family or society.

1. A skilled heart transplant physician who saves many people each week.
2. A plumber who's just trying to make ends meet.
3. An 88-year-old woman with Alzheimer's disease who is close to death.
4. An unborn child diagnosed with severe mental retardation with a life expectancy that could be as little as five years.
5. A six-million-dollar-a-year athlete who is the top name in his sport.

Allow each group to report briefly. As your students explain their answers, record the kinds of things by which they made their evaluations, such as, contribution to society, quality of life, talents and abilities. Write this list on newsprint or on the board.

In God's Image

After your students have had a chance to share their answers, direct their attention to Matthew 5:21–22.

Ask, "Why do you think Jesus is so harsh about placing judgment on others?" Give students a hint by telling them to look up Genesis 2:7 and Genesis 9:6. (Each person is made in God's image. When we place value judgments on people, we are judging the image which God has created, which He alone has the right to do. See also James 4:12.)

Redirect the students' attention to the text of Psalm 139. Ask your students to make a list of what every life has in common as described by this passage. As they share, make a second list on newsprint or on the board. (Possible answers might include these: created by God; He "knits" people together; fearfully and wonderfully made; His eyes saw the unformed body; He knew exactly what we would look like; and He knew every day of our lives before we lived the first one.) Continue, "If this is true, then what does this say about the physician, the plumber, the 88-year-old woman, the unborn child, and the athlete?" (Each is created by God's hand; each is fearfully and wonderfully made; God has ordained the days for each one of them. In short, each is valuable to God.) The problem is not that God has blessed some people with lives of value and cursed others. The problem is that we, imperfect people, have applied our own imperfect standards for what makes life valuable. Point out the difference between the two lists of qualities that give value to life. One lists human standards—a list of what we think is important. It is based on performance, wealth, talent, intellect, and things people do. The other list points out that life is valuable because of what God does. These are two totally different approaches to determining what really gives life value.

A Note for the Leader

The term "sanctity of life" is used frequently but not often defined. It means that life is sacred to God. Throughout the Scriptures, God claims exclusive ownership and management of all life, especially human life. Below is a list of just a few of those verses that are worth looking up to review God's sacred view of life: Deuteronomy 8:3; Deuteronomy 32:39; 1 Samuel 2:6; Job 34:14–15; Romans 4:17; James 4:15.

On first impression this is a confusing passage. Jesus is teaching about the value of a person. To say to someone "raca" was to call him or her empty headed or stupid. It was a judgment on the intellect, based on the person's actions. This kind of insult could be addressed by the Sanhedrin, or civil court. To say to someone "you fool" was to scorn a person's heart or character; it was to condemn him or her as unworthy of God's grace. It was to put one's self in God's place of judgment.

What's Your Approach?

Lay a six-foot to eight-foot two-by-four on the ground (or stretch out an eight-foot string) and ask for four volunteers. Have one pair stand facing the other at each end of the board or string. Give the following instructions: "The object is for each pair to get to the other end of this bridge without falling or stepping off. Both pairs must begin at the same time. Whoever gets to the other side without falling off wins." Direct them to start and watch what happens. Most likely it will become a competition to see who can remain on the longest. If time allows, let other pairs try. With a final set of volunteers, add this instruction: "This time let me clarify your goal. Everyone wins who makes it from one end to the other. The ideal is for both teams to make it across. You need to help each other." If additional help is needed, invite other students who are not on the teams to assist from the sides. Then debrief with an explanation like this one. "When the emphasis was on one team winning, one team tried to defeat the other team while others in the class sat back and watched. When the goal was for all to win, the teams worked together and helped one another. In order for all to win, sometimes it takes a lot of help. Your view of the value of life might similarly vary according to how you measure value. If value is measured by what you produce, earn, look like, or do, then life's value may shift, change, or vary from person to person. If life is valuable because God is the one who creates and sustains it, then its value doesn't change based on circumstances."

Seeing the Value

Unless you have extra time, choose this activity or the next one, but not both.

Read aloud to the class Acts 17:25–28. According to verse 28 it is in God that we "have our being", that is, it is God who gives our lives purpose. It is the fact that we are in God, that our lives are filled with His presence, that brings meaning to our lives, whatever the circumstances. Refer back to the opening life situations. Ask your group to consider the cases of the Alzheimer's victim and the unborn child. "From God's point of view, why is each of these people valuable? How can God's presence be experienced in each case?" After allowing a few moments for thought, use the following comments to assist class discussion.

Eighty-eight-year-old woman—Refer to the two-by-four exercise. It took people working together to get through the exercise, to reach each's goal. So in this woman's life a lot of help is needed to get through this tough time. Her situation is an opportunity for friends and family to work together to support her and each other in this eventually fatal disease. Though it can be a time-consuming and frustrating struggle, God calls us to respect His image in this woman by doing all we can to respect and support her life. Our goal is to help her see God's presence and loving care through our hands.

The unborn child—Just like it will take a lot of work to support the Alzheimer's victim, so it will be an effort to support this child and its family. Though his outward physical and mental abilities may be extremely limited, inside this child God has placed His image.

What I Could Do

Unless you have extra time, do this activity or the previous one, but not both.

Break your group into groups of three or four. Give each group one of the following situations. Ask group members how they could respond to each situation to promote God's view that each life is a precious gift in itself because it is created in His image. You might want to assign each group one situation or allow members of the group to pick whichever one interests them, or give your students the option of coming up with their own. Perhaps they are currently dealing with a real-life situation.

- An unwed pregnant teen at your school
- A friend's grandfather who is on life support after a stroke
- A friend of your mom's who is dying a painful death from cancer
- A classmate who is contemplating suicide

Give group members a few minutes to work together, then have a representative report to the class.

Closing

In their small groups, or as a class if you prefer, have students look back at Psalm 139:13–16. Have them reflect on how God has formed each of them as you read it aloud. Close in prayer by having each one pray something like this: "Dear God, I thank you that … (have student insert one of the phrases from the text) I am fearfully and wonderfully made" or "You know all my days" or "You knew from the beginning of time what I would become."

Many times teens look at people in tough life situations and conclude that God must not be in them, that those lives would be better off terminated. This is where passages such as Psalm 10:17–18; Psalm 146:5–9; and Romans 11:33–36 refocus our attention on the presence of God as the true source of a good life instead of worldly comfort, wealth, or deeds.

Power Play 7

Decisions

(Three copies of this script are needed.)

You created my inmost being; You knit me together in my mother's womb. I praise You because I am fearfully and wonderfully made; Your works are wonderful, I know that full well. (Psalm 139:13–14)

Summary

God has created us with great love and care. He is always with us, watching and guiding us. Life is a wondrous miracle to be celebrated!

Characters

- SPEAKER 1—an unborn child, can be either male or female
- SPEAKER 2—a doctor, male
- SPEAKER 3—a retired person, female

SPEAKER 1: I've known life for only 60 days now, but I haven't wasted one bit of time. Already I have eye sockets, and my fingers and toes are developing. And by the end of nine months, I'll be fully formed and ready to meet the world. My mother doesn't even know I exist yet, but I do exist just the same. The only One who knows me now is my Creator. He was with me at the beginning—at my conception. God has knit me together with such loving care and precision. And He has a wonderful life planned for me!

SPEAKER 2: I've wanted to be a doctor for a long time—not simply because of the money or the status. No, I honestly want to help people. I chose to specialize in obstetrics because I can't think of anything better than bringing a new life into the world. What an honor to be able to take part in such a miracle! It's also a great responsibility. Most nights, I find myself praying, "God, You are the great physician. Enable me to care for my patients as You would care for them." Yes, it's been a long road—year after year of schooling, internship, residency—but it paid off. I've finally been able to start my own practice. I'm thrilled at the prospect of what God has in store for me.

SPEAKER 3: I've spent the better part of my life working in one way or another. First I was an office manager. Then my husband Bill and I decided to start a family. I chose to be a full-time mother. *(She laughs.)* Anyone who says that parenting isn't a full-time job obviously has never been a parent! Just being able to keep track of all four of my children's different schedules was a major project, not to mention trying to fit a little time in for Bill. But I wouldn't have missed a minute of it. Well, my children are all grown now, with families of their own. My husband is about to retire, and we've decided that it's our turn to spend some time together. We've put aside a little nest egg, and now we're going to travel—nothing fancy, a few road trips, perhaps even to the Grand Canyon. You know, even though I was sad when my last child left home, I'm excited about this new chapter in my life—to be together with the wonderful husband God gave me! I know we have a great future ahead of us.

SPEAKER 1 *(sadly):* My mother knows about me now, but it wasn't the happy discovery I thought it would be. You see, I'm a surprise, to say the least. She keeps saying things like, "How could this happen? What am I going to do with it?" *It.* She calls me *it.* I know that she's shocked and confused, but doesn't she realize that I'm alive in here? I'm a person, just like she is. Some of her friends

50

have been telling her that she doesn't have to deal with "nine months of hell." They think she should abort me. They tell her it's her choice, and no one else's. But didn't she already make her choice when she decided to have sex? Aren't they forgetting about me? Just because I don't have a voice, they act as if I don't exist. Oh God, help me! You know that I'm here. You know who I'm supposed to be. Let my mother know too!

SPEAKER 2 *(angry):* I guess I was just naive to think that I could make my part of the world a better place. Maybe that's why I'm so disillusioned now. I want to bring life into the world. And now, I'm faced with a choice that goes against everything I stand for. A woman came into my office the other day and asked me to do a sonogram. She wanted to know the sex of the child she said. I was very happy to tell her that she was carrying a boy. I never expected her reaction. She burst into tears—not happy tears, but gut-wrenching sobs. She told me that she and her husband already had three sons and were trying for a girl. Then, very matter-of-factly, she asked me to abort the baby. I couldn't believe what I'd heard. I told her that I don't do abortions, and even if I did, I would never perform one as a matter of gender selection. She looked at me as if I'd just spit on her. "What kind of a doctor are you?" she demanded. Then she stormed out of my office. Now I'm receiving nasty telephone calls, even a threat to close down my practice. All those years of hard work and struggle seem to be for nothing just because I wouldn't bend on one issue. And now, I wonder, God, what kind of doctor am I?

SPEAKER 3 *(near tears):* Nothing turned out like we'd hoped it would. We never even made it to the Grand Canyon. A week into retirement, Bill had a stroke. He's been in a coma ever since. The doctors don't give us much hope. There are so many tubes and machines connected to him. I just don't know what to do. My oldest son thinks that we should let nature take its course. He says, "I know that Dad would want to die with dignity." None of the other children are willing to give any kind of advice. I don't blame them. I wish Bill and I had talked about this before, but we never did. I guess no one likes to face the fact that he or she will die someday. Oh, God, help me make this decision!

SPEAKER 1 *(happy):* Thank You, Lord, for hearing me! My mother has decided not to abort me. She'll carry me full term, and after I'm born, I'll be adopted by a Christian couple. In fact, she was able to pick them out herself at the agency. They've met and have promised to keep in touch so that she'll always know how I'm doing. One day, when I'm much older, I hope to meet my mother again and tell her thank you for remembering me—for allowing me to live!

SPEAKER 2 *(satisfied):* The answer to my question was in my heart all the time. I became a doctor to preserve human life, and to compromise my stand would be to compromise myself and everything I believe in. I will continue to do the work the Lord gave me to do, and nothing else. I only pray that one day, everyone in my profession will feel the same way.

SPEAKER 3: From a practical and financial viewpoint, turning off Bill's life support made sense—to the doctors, to some of my children, even, to some extent, to me. But in my heart, I knew that giving the okay to end life support would be the same as saying, "Go ahead, kill my husband." I couldn't do it. I prayed to God that He would end the lingering uncertainty. That He would either take Bill home to be with Him, or grant us a miracle and bring Bill back to his family. God heard my prayer—He gave us our miracle—Bill came out of the coma! He has a lot of rehab ahead of him, but he's alive. And he thanked us for waiting, for not giving up on him before his time was done. I thank God that He gave me the wisdom to make the right choice. What about you? What would you do if you were in my place and had the life of a loved one in your hands?

SPEAKER 2: What would you do if you were me and had to make a difficult choice between your moral convictions and how it might affect your entire future?

SPEAKER 1: And what if you had been me? A hopeful new life whose existance depends on the decisions of the world around you? What if there was nothing that you could do?

Scripture quotation: NIV ®
© 1995 CPH

God Created Sex!

Focus

Though God created the gift of sexuality, sin has tarnished His gift. Often unmarried teenagers are led to sin sexually through a progression of sexual intimacy. God not only forgives us for any sexual impurity but also empowers us to be sexually pure through faith in Jesus Christ.

Objectives

By the power of Christ at work through God's Word and the Spirit the students will

1. identify the progression of sexual intimacy;
2. affirm what God says about the gift of sexuality and how far to go before marriage;
3. rejoice in God's forgiveness for all sins, including sexual sins.

A Powerful Word for the Leader

For additional perspective on this topic a devotional study is available for the leader. It is "Positive Sexuality," unit 2, study 8, found in *Power Words: Devotional Studies for Youth Bible Study Leaders*, CPH 20-2629.

This Study at a Glance

Activity	Time	Materials
In Deeper Than You Think!	5 minutes	
Sexual Sin in the Bible	20 minutes	Bibles
Sizzlin' Sam's Roller Coaster Ride	15 minutes	Six copies of power play 8
The Faces of Sexual Sin Today	15 minutes	Copies of student page 10
Closing	5 minutes	

In Deeper Than You Think!

Ask, "Has your mother or someone ever said to you, 'You're in a lot deeper trouble than you think?'" If so, ask the students to recall specifics as to why they got into trouble. You might want to prime the students' thinking by recalling something from your teenage days which had got you into "deeper trouble" than you had first expected (e.g., skipping school). List some of the students' responses on newsprint or on the board.

Then say, "Sin can be like quicksand. Just as someone who is stuck in quicksand will sink in deeper as he or she wiggles and struggles, so sin often progresses, gets more complicated, and goes out of control as one continues in it. This can also be the case with sexual sin."

Sexual Sin in the Bible

Ask the students to look up in their Bibles the story of David, Bathesheba, and Uriah in 2 Samuel 11:1–5; 14–17; 26–27. Invite several volunteers to read these verses aloud. Then say, "Help me chart the progression of sin in this story." Write the following events on newsprint or on the board with arrows connecting each event to the next. (David sees Bathsheba bathing. In his lust for her *he invites her into his bedroom. They have sex.* She *conceives.* He tries to *cover up* his sin by putting *Uriah,* her husband, in the front line of battle where he is *killed.* David then *takes Bathsheba as his wife.*)

Ask, "Why would David sin in such a way? Wasn't he the man who killed Goliath with the strength given to him by God Himself? Wasn't he the one who was victorious over a ferocious lion? Didn't he pray to God, write about God, dedicate songs to God? Why did this man of God get into trouble?" (David was very human in that he sinned like everyone else. David got in trouble when he turned his eyes from God. The devil is always happiest when he can get people to focus on the wrong things in life.)

Ask a volunteer to read aloud James 1:14–15. Ask, "What is the progression of sin according to these words?" As the students spell out the progression, list the steps on the board. (Sin is conceived or thought of, then it is put into action, and finally, the sin can give birth to spiritual death.)

Ask the students, "As David looked at the woman he wanted, one person stood in his way, Uriah. David chose to get rid of Uriah. What other choices did he have?" (David could have simply confessed his sin and asked for forgiveness from God, Uriah, and Bathsheba. He could have honored God's will stating, "This woman belongs to Uriah. I will respect that relationship!")

Ask, "In what way does God stand in our way at times when we want to do something wrong?" (Through His Word, God convicts us and reminds us of what is right and wrong. Through His Word the Holy Spirit also empowers us to do God's will.)

Ask a volunteer to read aloud 1 Corinthians 6:18–20. Remind the students that the analogy of being "bought at a price" comes from a custom during Paul's time. Earthly slaves could pay a price for liberty into a god's temple, and thus, become the god's property, free from their earthly masters. God has purchased us from sin, death, and the power of the devil through the life, death, and resurrection of His Son, Jesus Christ. He has not only purchased us but He has set up residency in us. His Holy Spirit dwells within us. Ask, "Since we belong to Him, what can we do with the power of the Holy Spirit dwelling within us whenever sin rears its ugly head?" (We can with the power of the Holy Spirit overcome the power of Satan. Sin can be overcome.)

Sizzlin' Sam's Roller Coaster Ride

Present power play 8. Follow it with this discussion.

Ask volunteers to match events in power play 8, "Sizzlin Sam's Roller Coaster Ride," with stages in the progression of sexual intimacy. (Robert and Melinda's journey to sexual intercourse is compared to a roller coaster ride. Just as it's hard to get off a roller coaster ride once you've gotten on, so it's hard to stop the progression of sexual feelings each time physical intimacy is increased.)

Write on the board these lines from the power play: hold hands to get started; the Kissin' Vertical Loop; the Neckin' Cyclone Ascent; Pettin' Hill; and the Final Step. Ask, "How do these phrases describe the progression of sexual sin?" (Sexual intimacy often progresses along these lines: holding hands; kissing; necking; petting; sexual intercourse.)

The Faces of Sexual Sin Today

Distribute copies of student page 10. Remind the students that it's easy to get caught up in what everyone else is doing or what "comes naturally!" Ask students to reread 1 Corinthians 6:18–20 and review the chart "The Progression of Sexual Intimacy." Give the students time to mark or write responses to the statements on the student page. Allow volunteers to share their responses. Then ask, "Considering what Paul says in 1 Corinthians 6:18–20, how far do you think is *too far* to go when dating a boyfriend or girlfriend? Explain your answer."

Be careful not to come across too legalistic at this point. Don't judge the students harshly for their answers. Instead, keep lovingly returning them to the Word of God to do its work of convicting sinners. Remind them of God's love and the forgiveness He gives through the blood of Jesus Christ. Remind them also of the strength God provides through His Word and Spirit to help them resist sin of all kinds.

Closing

Challenge each student to spend a moment in prayer to God. Encourage each student to pray not only for himself or herself but also for the other students in the class. Assure the students that their prayers are only between themselves and God. Ask them to use the format that follows for their prayer (write the format on the board).

Lord God, thank You for the gift of sexuality. Forgive me for the times I have misused this gift. I recall specifically … (silently confess specific sins). Help me to … (ask God for help). In the name of Jesus Christ. Amen.

God Created Sex!

Indicate your reaction to the following statements or write your own.

1. "Don't worry. Nothing can happen. You have a seat belt! It'll protect you!"
   a. "But what if it doesn't work?"
   b. "Take your seat belt and your ride. I'm getting off."
   c. "Yeah, seat belts do provide ultimate safety!"
   d. _____

2. "Melinda, honey, you said you love me. If you really do, you'll take this ride with me."
   a. "If you really loved me, you wouldn't ask me to take this ride!"
   b. "I love you too much to take this ride with you."
   c. "Take a hike, bud!"
   d. _____

3. "Don't worry, honey; this will be fun."
   a. "I can hardly wait!"
   b. "Fun? Define it for me."
   c. "Don't *you* worry, honey; we're history."
   d. _____

4. "It's the natural thing to do."
   a. "You mean like animals?"
   b. "But does that make it right?"
   c. "Not for me, nature boy. I'm getting off."
   d. _____

5. "I don't feel well ... I feel like ... like I'm going to throw up!"
   a. "Sure, go ahead."
   b. "I love you but get away from me."
   c. "What can I do to help?"
   d. _____

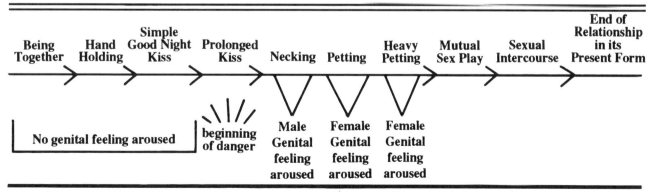

*Chart from Patricia B. Driscoll. *Sexual Common Sense: Affirming Adolescent Abstinence.* Womanity Publications.

© 1995 CPH

Power Plays 2, Student Page 10

Power Play 8

Sizzlin' Sam's Roller Coaster Ride

(Six copies of this script are needed.)

But each one is tempted when, by his own evil desire, he is dragged away and enticed. Then, after desire has conceived, it gives birth to sin; and sin, when it is full-grown, gives birth to death. (James 1:14–15)

Summary

As physical intimacy increases, so does the progression of sexual feeling. James speaks of this progression in James 1:14–15. Robert and Melinda's journey to sexual intercourse is compared to a roller coaster ride. Just as it's hard to get off a roller coaster ride once you've gotten on, so it's hard to stop the progression of sexual feelings each time physical intimacy is increased.

Characters

- *GATE ATTENDANT—the attendant who collects the tickets and helps those who want to ride on the roller coaster
- *SIZZLIN' SAM—the voice who seduces and tells the riders what they can expect with each hill and curve
- ROBERT—the boyfriend
- MELINDA—the girlfriend
- PASSENGER 1—a young man seated behind Robert and Melinda
- PASSENGER 2—the girlfriend of PASSENGER 1
- * GATE ATTENDANT and SAM can be the same person.

Props (Optional)

- Cassette tape player with recorded carnival-like music
- Four chairs placed two in front, two in back, all four facing audience
- Microphone or cardboard megaphone
- Some tickets

GATE ATTENDANT: Welcome! So you've come to ride the Sizzlin' Sam's Roller Coaster. Congratulations. This is better than any other roller coaster ride you've been on, even better than the famous Coney Island Cyclone or the Screaming Eagle. It's a ride you'll never forget.

ROBERT: Yeah! I hear it's awesome. Some friends told me all about it! Said it's unbelievable! *(He winks at the GATE ATTENDANT and whispers to him.)* Actually, my friends in the locker room dared me.

GATE ATTENDANT: Why did you wait so long? Too chicken?

ROBERT: Well, actually, I guess I wasn't ready. But I'm not going to wait any longer. All my friends told me they have been on this ride—lots of times. If I don't go, they'll think there's something wrong with me ... like I'm some kind of wimp ... or worse!

GATE ATTENDANT: Never! You don't want them laughing at you! ... or teasing you! ... or, worse yet, thinking there's something ... *(clears his throat) wrong* with you!

ROBERT: Yeah! *(Almost as if she were an afterthought, he adds:)* Oh yeah, this is Melinda, my girlfriend. *(He points to MELINDA.)*

GATE ATTENDANT: Hi! This is your lucky day, babe! *(He laughs in a villianous way.)* Take this ride and you'll never want to ride any more of those baby rides! This one will satisfy your every need!

MELINDA: Bob, I don't think I want to go. I don't think ... I'm ready.

ROBERT: Melinda, honey, you said you love me. If you really do, you'll take this ride with me. If you don't come along, I'll take someone else!

MELINDA *(hesitantly)*: Okay, but ...

GATE ATTENDANT *(finishing MELINDA's sentence)*: But don't worry. Nothing can happen. You have a seat belt! It'll protect you! *(Aside)* When it doesn't break!

ROBERT: Great.

GATE ATTENDANT: That'll be 10 tickets each.

ROBERT: Wow. That's all I've got. Is this ride expensive!

GATE ATTENDANT *(aside)*: If you only knew!

(ROBERT and MELINDA get into the chairs. PASSENGERS 1 and 2 are already seated.)

56

SIZZLIN' SAM *(seductively)*: Welcome, fellow sinners … *(clearing his throat)* I mean, *riders!* I'm Seductive … *(once again clears his throat, realizing he has made a mistake)* uh, Sizzlin' Sam. Though you won't be able to see me, I'll be your guide during your brief trip on the Sizzlin' Sam's Roller Coaster ride. Without any further ado, let's get started. Buckle up! It's all you have to worry about! That little belt will keep you from gettin' hurt!

(ROBERT and MELINDA pretend to put on their seat belts.)

ROBERT *(to passenger in seat behind him)*: This is the first time I've ever been on this ride. How about you?

PASSENGER 1: No. I've been here lots of times. The only thing that changes is the person I ride with! I believe in sharing the pleasure of my company! *(He laughs in a villainous way.)*

ROBERT *(aside)*: Sounds great!

SIZZLIN' SAM: Hang on, we're ready to take off. It'll help if you hold hands to get started.

(ROBERT and MELINDA hold each other's hands.)

SIZZLIN' SAM: We'll be ascending slowly. Just sit back and enjoy the clickity-clack sounds of the lift chain as it pulls you closer and closer to each other and toward that first drop.

(ROBERT smiles at MELINDA and then puts his arm around her as they sway gently to the left.)

ROBERT: Don't worry, honey; this will be fun.

SIZZLIN' SAM: Get ready for what we call the Kissin' Vertical Loop.

ROBERT: Whoa, this is hot!!

SIZZLIN' SAM: That's right … holdin' hands … kissin' lips … makes for the start of a great sizzlin' time!

MELINDA: Wow! I guess this isn't going to be so bad after all! But are we ever movin'!

SIZZLIN' SAM: That's the way we like it … reckless, out of control! Get ready to experience the Neckin' Cyclone Ascent. The twists and turns are unsurpassed in the coaster world!

ROBERT and MELINDA: This is moving way too fast. Can we stop?

SIZZLIN' SAM *(laughing)*: Of course not! Get ready! You're heading to the Ridge of Danger, also known as Pettin' Hill.

MELINDA: Wait! I want to stop! Robert, why did you make me go on this ride?

ROBERT: Because you love me, that's why! This is really what love is all about! It's the natural thing to do.

SIZZLIN' SAM: That's right! It's natural! Do what feels natural. It's being free. It's being an adult. It's being grown up. That's what we believe at Sizzlin' Sam's.

MELINDA: But it's getting dangerously close to … well … *(clears her throat)* you know, Robert … *(She's scared to go on.)*

ROBERT: Yes. Yes. Yes! To being a real man!

MELINDA: What does all this have to do with being a man?

ROBERT: Women just don't understand.

(ROBERT and MELINDA lurch to the right.)

ROBERT and MELINDA: Whoa!

ROBERT: Look how fast we're movin'! Close your eyes, Melinda. We're going to be reaching the Final Step soon!

SIZZLIN' SAM: Here it comes! This is what life is all about! It's what everyone talks about!

ROBERT *(both are holding on to each other)*: Whoa!! This could easily become an addiction!

MELINDA *(putting her head on ROBERT'S shoulder)*: I don't feel well … I feel like … like I'm going to throw up!

ROBERT *(pushing her away)*: Well, get away from me. I don't want to get all messed up!

MELINDA: But, Robert! I thought you loved me!

Scripture quotation: NIV®
© 1995 CPH

9

Me First?

Focus

Our sinful nature wants to keep our time, talents, and treasures for our own enjoyment and use. God sees things differently. He gives us many blessings so that we might serve Him and others who are in need. He sent His only Son to be our suffering Savior. By humbling Himself to die for us, Jesus has demonstrated the true nature of servanthood and calls us, by the power of the Holy Spirit, to serve as His hands, feet, and heart in our world.

Objectives

By the power of Christ at work through His Word and Spirit the students will

1. identify ways in which they can be of service to others;
2. desire to serve others out of love and gratitude for Christ's acts of service and sacrifice for them;
3. become involved in and committed to acts of service in their home, church, school, and community.

This Study at a Glance

Activity	Time	Materials
Opener	5 minutes	
The Youth Group That Lost (and Gained) Everything	10 minutes	Four copies of power play 9
*God's Word	20 minutes	Index cards with Bible verses, basket or box, Bibles, copies of student page 11
I'd Love to Help, But …	20 minutes	Copies of student page 11
Closing	5 minutes	

*Advance preparation or special supplies required.

Opener

Ask, "How much money do we have together?" Direct everyone (including yourself) to empty pockets and purses and count the cash. Ask, "What could we do with that amount of money?" List responses on the board.

The Youth Group That Lost (and Gained) Everything

Introduce the play, which focuses on a youth group that had over $600 in its treasury and was faced with a tough decision. Present the play at this time.

After the play, discuss the following questions.

1. What did the youth group lose in this experience? ($600.)

2. What did group members gain? (They gained the satisfaction of knowing they had carried out Jesus' command to love one another; a stronger faith in God's promise to provide for their own needs; the approval of their heavenly Father, who rejoices when His children, by the power of the Holy Spirit, follow in the footsteps of their Savior.)

Then suggest, "God has plans for us too."

God's Word

Ask the students to think about their futures. What does each of them hope to do or be? Then say, "Raise your hand if you are thinking about becoming a doctor. How about a teacher? a pilot?" (Name a few more high profile choices.) "All right. Now, honestly, how many of you really have your heart set on becoming a butler? a maid? Why not?

"Dedicating your life to waiting on others hand and foot hardly seems very glamorous or profitable. Being a servant isn't really a lot of fun. It involves doing boring, often disgusting tasks merely for the purpose of helping someone else. Do servants ever get the appreciation and recognition they deserve? Of course not. Part of being a servant involves blending into the background so the one who is served looks good.

"Do servants make a lot of money? Not usually—unless they betray their masters by writing a kiss-and-tell book about his or her business. And why should one person call another human person *master*? How humiliating! Who would ever want to be a servant, *anyway*?

"Yet, just read what Jesus suggests in Luke 22:27. What role does Jesus willingly take on?" (He came to serve.)

Divide the class into groups of three or four. Give each group index cards, with these Bible passages written on them: John 13:3–5 (washing feet); Matthew 9:27–29 (healing the blind); Matthew 14:18–20 (feeding 5,000 hungry people); Mark 4:35–39 (calming a frightening storm); Mark 10:13–16 (defending and blessing little children); John 10:11–18 (taking care of His sheep); John 17:1 (praying for His people); John 11:38–44 (raising the dead); Luke 23:26–46 (dying for us). Put the cards into a basket or box. A member of each team draws a card, reads the passage, and then acts out or draws (on newsprint or on the board) the act of service Jesus is performing in that verse. The other classmates are then to guess what that act of service is. Groups could do this activity alternately or at the same time.

Then discuss:

- "Why did Jesus do all these things?" (He loved us.)
- "What does Matthew 20:28 tell us about Jesus' whole purpose on earth?" (He came to serve and give His life as a ransom for many.)

Mark 1:21–35, 45 tells about a typical day for Jesus. Have a student read the verses while you write on newsprint or on the board all Jesus did during those few hours. (He taught in the synogogue, healed a man who was possessed by a demon, visited with Peter's family, healed Peter's mother-in-law, and then spent a "quiet" evening at home healing the crowd of people who gathered at the door.)

A Powerful Word for the Leader

For additional perspective on this topic a devotional study is available for the leader. It is "When Is Enough?" unit 2, study 9, found in *Power Words: Devotional Studies for Youth Bible Study Leaders,* CPH 20-2629.

Then say, "Jesus' day was as busy as some of yours. Didn't He ever get tired? What kept Him going and going and going? Well, of course, He was God. He had divine resources. When we are tired or discouraged, we have divine resources too. God continues to serve and refresh us often through the service of others. When someone needs our help, even if we feel he or she doesn't deserve it, God through His undeserved love strengthens us to serve. Ask God to give us that spirit of humble, compassionate service.

"The apostle Paul gives us another clue. Read his encouraging words in Galatians 6:9. We can't give up, he says, because we have a harvest to reap. What kind of harvest is Paul talking about? (A harvest of souls—believers in Jesus.) Jesus is counting on us and all His servants to spread His Word so that many souls will be led to believe in Him through the Holy Spirit and will be made a part of His family forever. We have been part of that harvest. The Holy Spirit used someone to bring us to faith and work new life in us through that faith in Christ. Now we have the opportunity to join in the harvesting.

"How do you let people know what Jesus is like? You may tell and show them. You put on the same attitude Jesus had and let Him serve others through you. 1 John 3:16–18 says it all." (Read the passage together, if possible.) "By dying for our sin, removing its weight, and being new life in us, Jesus empowers us to sacrifice for others.

"Think about people in your family, church, or community who need help." Encourage students to suggest specific names of people. Write their names on a chalkboard or large sheet of newsprint. Discuss ways the class can work together to make a difference.

Distribute copies of student page 11. Direct students to the first section. Say, "Think of one specific person you know who needs Jesus' loving touch. Substitute that person's name and your name in appropriate places in these verses": This is how *(person in need)* know[s] what love is: Jesus Christ laid down His life for *(person in need)*. And *(your name)* ought to lay down *(his/her)* life for *(person in need)*. If *(your name)* has material possessions and sees *(person in need)* in need but has no pity on *(him/her)*, how can the love of God be in *(your name)*? Dear *(your name)*, let us not love with words or tongue but with actions and in truth. (1 John 3:16–18)

"God does, indeed, love us with more than words. He showed the extent of His love by giving His Son to die on the cross. Now He empowers us to give our lives too in the service of others. If you offer to help because someone pays you or because you feel guilty if you don't, then you are not serving God by your actions. You are merely a hired hand; not a loving servant. But when the Spirit of God is at work in your heart, He helps you to give as He has given to you—fully, freely, gladly."

Direct each person to choose a need from the list on the board and plan how to help in that area. Make specific plans right away to put these ideas into action. Ask each student to initial the project on which he or she will act. Copy the list and ask next week how the act of service is progressing.

I'd Love to Help, But ...

Point out to the students that most acts of giving fall into three categories: giving of your time, giving of your talent, and giving of your money. Ask, "Which of these three is the easiest for you? Which is the hardest? Why?" Discuss examples of each kind of giving (time, talent, money). Then, direct the class to the chart on the student page.

Introduce the chart by saying, "Sometimes our service to others is hindered by our lack of time. We are too busy to see the needs of others, too busy to care, too busy to respond. Analyze your use of time by estimating the average amount of time you spend each week in the activities on the chart." Give the students a few moments to do this. Then say, "Is your time in balance, or do you overdo some aspects of your life? If you wanted to, could you find more time for helping others? Try readjusting your schedule. What could you change?" Allow a few moments for the students to complete the "Future" column of the chart.

Closing

Hold hands and stand in a circle while you pray. The teacher begins: "Dear Father, we thank You for Your undeserved love for us. You know exactly what we need, and You care for us in every way. We pray, now, for others who need Your help." (Take turns around the circle just calling out names of people who are in need. Keep going several times around the group until no more names are mentioned.) "Lord, You know the needs of these persons we have mentioned. You love them, as You love us, with a perfect love, and You have the power to provide for them. Use us, Lord, as Your instruments in answering our prayer. Hug others with our arms; support others with our dollars; feed others with our cupboards; hear others through our ears; comfort others with our tears; love others with our hearts; bring others into Your family through our words; serve others through our lives. For You have given us everything in Christ Jesus, our Lord. Amen."

Extending the Lesson

Take up an extra collection right now and use the money to help someone in need.

Undertake a larger project. Assign someone to look into paying support for a child in a poverty-stricken land or visiting a nursing home. Explore other ways to serve. The important thing is to decide on something specific and take immediate action. Don't just talk about it; do it.

Challenge the students to do one or more of these next week:

- Think of a person whom you do not like. Pray for him or her. Find an opportunity to be of help to that person without anyone ever finding out.
- Often it is hardest to be a willing servant in our own homes. Do an act of kindness today for each member of your family.
- Thank God for His undeserved love for you. Pray that He will work in you a desire to serve others in His name.

Me First?

1 John 3:16–18—Up Close and Personal

"This is how _(person in need)_ know[s] what love is: Jesus Christ laid down His life for _(person in need)_. And _(your name)_ ought to lay down _(his/her)_ life for _(person in need)_. If _(your name)_ has material possessions and sees _(person in need)_ in need but has no pity on _(him/her)_, how can the love of God be in _(your name)_? Dear _(your name)_, let us not love with words or tongue but with actions and in truth."

I'd Love to Help, But ...

How do you spend the time you have? In the "Now" column estimate how many hours of a typical week you spend in each of the following activities:

Activity	Now	Future?
School		
Homework		
Eating		
Talking on phone		
TV		
Activities with family members		
Church		
Youth group		
Sleeping		
Reading the Bible		
Daydreaming		
Exercising/playing		
Bathing and personal care		
Doing chores		
Helping others		
Other		

Now dream about how you'd like it to be. If you could rearrange your time, how would it be spent differently? Estimate changes in the "Future" column.

Scripture quotation: NIV®
© 1995 CPH

Power Plays 2, Student Page 11

 **Power Play 9**

The Youth Group That Lost (and Gained) Everything

(Four copies of this script are needed.)

This is how we know what love is: Jesus Christ laid down His life for us. And we ought to lay down our lives for our brothers. If anyone has material possessions and sees his brother in need but has no pity on him, how can the love of God be in him? Dear children, let us not love with words or tongue, but with actions and in truth. (1 John 3:16–18)

Summary
The love of Christ is active and unconditional sacrifice. As we live in His forgiveness (grace) and strength, we are able to love one another. With Jesus' love in our hearts, life is real!

Characters
- JON—the youth group president; a leader, struggling
- AMANDA—searching
- JOSH—passionate, funny
- MOLLY—unsettled by conflict

Setting
A classroom or living room

Props (Optional)
Four chairs arranged to form a half-circle facing the audience.

JON: Now that was one strange person. How did he get in, anyway?

AMANDA: Who invited him?

MOLLY: Don't look at me. He sure was quiet—until he made his pitch.

JON: Well, have a seat everybody. We need to talk. *(Everyone casually sits down.)*

MOLLY: Maybe we should get the pastor in on this.

JON: We already know what he'd say.

JOSH: That's true. This guy's family needs money for next month's rent. So we do a car wash and help him out, right?

JON: Maybe. But we don't even know the guy. What if next month I come in and say I need $600 for a new stereo system. Do I get a car wash too?

MOLLY: Come on, Jon. That's different!

JON: Well, I'm sorry, but what do we know about this guy?

JOSH: He's a loner at school. I've got him in one of my classes.

MOLLY: I think he's weird.

AMANDA: You don't know that, Molly.

JON: I think we have to be careful with our money. We can't throw it away for a lost cause. Can we even trust the guy?

MOLLY: And if we pay the rent this month, do we pay it next month too?

JOSH: Was anybody listening? He said it was just this month, that his dad is behind on child-support payments. They just moved here. He only needs $600.

JON: Only? We have $612.93 in our youth group treasury. Is that a coincidence or what?

AMANDA: Shouldn't the rest of the group be here talking about this?

JON: We can make a suggestion about what we should do. They elected us for stuff like this.

JOSH: I think we should take the money out of the treasury, give away the $600, and have a party on the rest. Then we can declare ourselves bankrupt and start all over again.

JON: Funny, Josh.

JOSH: I'm serious. I can't believe we're even discussing this.

MOLLY: So, we raised all that money selling Christmas cards and working the fair booth, and he comes in and gets it? What happens when we need it for the national gathering?

JOSH: We have time to raise more money.

MOLLY: I do feel sorry for him. What did he say—he has two little brothers? It must be tough, but …

JOSH: "But!" I knew it! But what?

MOLLY: But we don't even know him. He's not part of our group. I mean, we'll probably never see him again!

AMANDA: Maybe Pastor has more information. I'll call him and ask. Be back in a minute. (*She exits.*)

JON: It's throwing money away.

MOLLY: He could look somewhere else for help.

JOSH: This is unbelievable. How can you guys *not* want to do this? I'm the treasurer. I could fill out a withdrawal slip and get the money tomorrow after school.

JON: Hold on, Josh. No one said you could do that. People helped us raise that money for the youth gathering, not for someone's rent. If you withdraw that money on your own, I'll resign as president.

JOSH: Hold that money *back,* Jon, and I'll quit the group.

MOLLY: I just wish we didn't have to talk about this. Look at what it's doing to us.

JON (*to JOSH*): What makes you think you're so right?

JOSH: My gut, okay? I feel it in my gut.

JON: So we drain the treasury to satisfy your gut. Maybe we should just feed it instead.

AMANDA (*enters*): Well guys, here's the scoop.

JON: You got the pastor at home?

MOLLY: What did he say, Amanda?

AMANDA: He said that Robert—the guy who was here—and his family just moved here. His mom's looking for work. He's cooking at fast food. All they need is $600 for next month's rent. After that, things should settle down, but there are no guarantees. So, what Robert told us *is* true.

JON: Why can't the church help them out? They have a fund for stuff like this, don't they?

AMANDA: He *did* say we could ask the church to take care of it, but …

JOSH: Yeah, go on.

AMANDA: But, Robert didn't ask the *church*. He asked *us*.

MOLLY: So what did Pastor say we should do?

AMANDA: Like Jon said, you can almost guess what he'd say. He said, "Do what Jesus would do."

JON: And we all know what Jesus would do? Don't we?

AMANDA: Do we?

JON (*reluctantly*): He'd give him the $600 bucks. Jesus was always doing that kind of thing. (*He pauses.*) So why is it so hard to do? What makes it so hard for me to say, "Let's give him the money?"

MOLLY: It's a tough choice.

AMANDA: So what are we going to do?

JON: Let's call the rest of the group, fill them in, and do what the group votes to do. You know, I think they'll go for it.

JOSH: I can live with that.

AMANDA: Me too.

MOLLY: What about the party? Do you think Jesus would have thrown a party with what's left?

JON: I have to admit, that also sounds like something He might have done.

MOLLY: Then I hope we have the party too.

JON: We'll ask the group.

JOSH: That would leave us a nice round figure in the account—zero.

JON: I guess we'll just start over. Wow, this is hard for me.

JOSH: Same group. Same president. We'll just be broke.

AMANDA: That sounds like a plan. I think this will work out.

JON: Yeah, me too! Well, Josh, let's skip to refreshments and reward that gut of yours.

(*All exit.*)

Scripture quotation: NIV®
© 1995 CPH

My Music—To God's Glory!

10

This Study at a Glance

Activity	Time	Materials
Let's Talk about Music	10 minutes	
Pure, Lovely, Admirable?	10 minutes	Bibles
Music and Its Influence	15 minutes	Five copies of power play 10
Messages in Music	15 minutes	
So What?	10 minutes	

Let's Talk about Music

Say, "Today we're going to focus on music. I'd like you to say the first thing that comes to mind as I ask you a series of questions." (Record student responses on newsprint or on the board, putting the responses to the odd-numbered questions on the left and the responses to the even-numbered questions on the right.)

1. Think of a popular song today that speaks of love. What sorts of things does it say about love?
2. Name some things God says about love in His Holy Word.
3. List some memorable phrases you've heard in rap music.
4. What were some of the more memorable words spoken by Jesus in His famous Sermon on the Mount?
5. When you think of Madonna, what comes to your mind?
6. When you think of Mary Magdalene, what comes to your mind?

Don't be surprised to discover that the students know more about what popular music says about love than what Scripture says, or more about Madonna than Mary Magdalene. Point out, if it's true, that they seem to know more about music than Scripture. If this is true, ask why.

Pure, Lovely, Admirable?

Remind the students that as Christians we desire to bring honor to God in all that we do, including the music we listen to. When we

Focus

In the eyes of God, music is never "neutral." At times, our music brings honor to God. At other times, it dishonors Him with messages that are contrary to His Word. Even Christians sometimes listen to music that dishonors God, music that influences us negatively. We rejoice in knowing that our gracious God forgives us all our sins, including our sin of dishonoring Him with our music. God not only forgives us but He guides and empowers us with His Holy Word to select music that will bring Him glory.

Objectives

By the power of Christ at work through His Word and Spirit the students will

1. acknowledge the influence of music—both positive and negative;
2. affirm the need to use God's Word as a guide to selecting music;
3. give thanks to God for His forgiveness through Jesus Christ when we fail to honor Him with our music;
4. pray that He would reveal His will to us in the area of music through His Holy Word.

A Powerful Word for the Leader

For additional perspective on this topic a devotional study is available for the leader. It is "Music and Its Influence," unit 2, study 10, found in *Power Words: Devotional Studies for Youth Bible Study Leaders,* CPH 20-2629.

allow anything to direct our attention away from God and His will for us, we sin.

Ask the students to look up Philippians 4:4–5, 8. Invite a volunteer to read the passage aloud. Then ask, "What are some of the specific things Paul tells us to do in these verses?" (Rejoice in the Lord; let your gentleness be evident to all; whatever is true, whatever is noble, whatever is right, whatever is pure, whatever is lovely, whatever is admirable—if anything is excellent or praiseworthy—think about such things.)

Ask, "God tells us to think about good things. Why do impure things sometimes seem more exciting or interesting? Why doesn't God want us to think about those things? Is God against fun? Didn't He create sex for people to enjoy?" (God is a God of fun, but He's also an all-knowing God who knows what's best for His people. Though He created sex, God knows that the wrong use of sex can damage a person physically and spiritually. Satan is the one who tempts us to think about those things that are harmful, not God.)

Ask, "Why do you think songwriters include impure subjects or language in their music?" (Be prepared for obvious and deeper responses. Listen carefully and react slowly. Some students may point out that songwriters try to accurately portray the circumstances, attitudes, and language of real people with deep emotions. Some may also admit that sex and violence appeal to the rebel in us and sell recordings so that the songwriter makes money.)

Finally ask, "What impact do negative themes and language in music have on the listener?" (Don't work for closure, but lead into the next section.)

Music and Its Influence

Direct a reading or performance of power play 10. At its conclusion, ask the students to recall lines that struck them as important or true.

> Douglas Miller's argument that the music he listens to does not negatively influence him, "It's only music, Mom! No one listens to the words!"
>
> Dr. Geraldoman's parting comment, "I need to go to Deno's Donut Shop now, for one of Deno's special 'pick-me-up' donuts!"

Ask, "Why do advertisers spend thousands of dollars for a 30-second commercial if it's not going to influence a certain number of people to buy their product?" (The truth is, commercials do work. For every dollar spent, companies expect greater profits in return.) "If commericials have an influence, won't music have an influence too?" (The truth is, music does have an influence.)

Messages in Music

Ask each student to spend a few minutes writing down the words of their favorite song. After they've done this, ask them to reread Philippians 4:4–5, 8. With pen in hand ask them to cross out any words or phrases from their favorite song that do not fit the description given by Paul. Have them circle those that fit Paul's words. Invite the students to share what they discovered. Some of them may happily report that they didn't have to cross out any of the words in their song. Others may report minor or even major deletions. Whatever the situation, do not embarrass any of the students or scold them. Instead, let God's Word work: first to convict through the Law and then forgive through the Gospel.

Invite the students to close their eyes and to think again about the music they listen to. As they sit with their eyes closed, ask them to ask God for forgiveness for any songs which they've listened to which may not have brought honor to God. After a short while conclude with a prayer like this: "Dear Jesus, You paid for our sins. Thank You for the gift of forgiveness for which You paid. Continue to strengthen and guide us in choosing music that will bring You honor and be a positive influence in our lives. Amen."

Remind the students that the power to make good choices in our lives comes from God at work in us through faith in Christ. As we hear God's Word, especially the good news that Christ has won forgiveness of our sins through His death, we are strengthened in our faith and made new—strengthened to oppose sin and serve God.

So What?

Before they leave, invite the students to do one of the following activities this week:

1. Meet together with their families and critique the music each family member listens to. Be open and honest with one another. Pray together that God would help you as a family to give honor to God in your choices in music.

2. Find and listen to a Christian radio station. Listen each day. Does it bring you more peace than the music you were listening to before you tuned in? Does it meet the criteria of Philippians 4:4–5, 8?

Conclude by saying, "Words have power. The words in music also influence either positively or negatively. Satan seeks to influence us negatively through music. God works in us through His Word and Spirit so that we can examine the music we listen to and judge it according to God's Word. Though we may fail at times to bring God honor with our music, our gracious God forgives us and empowers us to be more obedient to His will."

Power Play 10
Music and Its Influence

(Five copies of this script are needed.)

Stop listening to instruction, my son, and you will stray from the words of knowledge. (Proverbs 19:27)

Characters

- ANNOUNCER—the one who introduces the host as well as speaks the advertisements
- DR. BLAKE GERALDOMAN—the host
- MRS. MILLER—a mother who is distraught over the music her son listens to
- DOUGLAS MILLER—the son of Mrs. Miller; he likes rap and heavy metal music
- STUDIO GUEST—someone who is in the audience of the Dr. Geraldoman Show
- (The studio audience could be represented by two or more actors or by those watching the play.)

Setting
A talk-show program

Props (Optional)

- Two chairs
- A real or toy microphone
- Several chairs for the audience

ANNOUNCER: Welcome to the Dr. Geraldoman Show. Today we're going to discuss music and its influence. It promises to be an exciting show! But first, let's welcome our esteemed host, the talk-show sensation everyone's talking about and listening to, the one and only, Dr. Blake Geraldoman. *(Applause.)*

DR. GERALDOMAN: Thank you! Thank you! Indeed, you are honored to have me in your city today. For our show we have with us Mrs. Miller and her son, Douglas. Mrs. Miller called us recently to say that she felt the music her son was listening to was harmful. Her son claims otherwise. We'll hear their story right after this commercial.

ANNOUNCER: Are you tired, enervated, exhausted and weary, disillusioned and disheartened? If so, stop at Deno's Donut Shop and pick up some of Deno's new special-energizing, delicious, delectable, delightful donuts! These donuts aren't ordinary donuts. They're Deno's donuts! They contain a special secret filling that is not only scrumptious but is also saturated with a sensational, succulent, sugary substance that simply energizes in a superhuman way!

DR. GERALDOMAN: We're going to start today by asking Mrs. Miller *(turns to Mrs. Miller)*, What are your objections to your son's music? What's so bad about it?

MRS. MILLER: The music my son listens to is nothing more than trash! It talks about suicide and rape, getting drunk, using drugs, smoking marijuana, treating women as sex objects, pillaging … you name it! One music video I saw showed a young girl no more than 16 years old being gang-raped by a group of sadistic bikers. It made me sick! One of the songs he likes has more foul language in it than I've heard in a lifetime.

DOUGLAS MILLER: If it's so bad, why do you listen to it?

MRS. MILLER: What choice do I have? You play it so loud I can hear it in every room of the house!

DOUGLAS MILLER: It's only music, Mom! No one listens to the words! I like the beat! Everyone listens to it!

MRS. MILLER: I don't care if everyone in the world listens to it. I don't like *you* listening to it.

DR. GERALDOMAN: Well, first of all, let's check it out! Douglas, does your music use foul language?

68

DOUGLAS MILLER: It depends on how you define *foul!* To me it's not foul! Mostly, I don't even listen to the words. I listen to the beat of the music!

DR. GERALDOMAN: You see, Mrs. Miller? So maybe what you hear and what your son hears are two different things.

MRS. MILLER: No way! Have you ever heard the words to some of the rap music kids are listening to today? It's disgusting! They're about everything from gang-rape to how to kill a cop.

DOUGLAS MILLER: I know where to draw the line! You haven't seen me go out and attempt suicide, have you, Mom?

MRS. MILLER: But it can happen! The Bible says, "As [a person] thinks … so is he" (Proverbs 23:7 KJV).

DOUGLAS MILLER: Okay, Mom! If that's so, let's talk about your music—that junk you force me to listen to whenever I'm with you in the car.

MRS. MILLER: There's nothing wrong with country music!

DOUGLAS MILLER: Right! What about the song I heard yesterday? It said something about going to the bar to cry in one's beer, because home was such a burden. This guy was singing about how his wife cramped his style! And if I remember correctly, God was smiling on the whole scene, because He was, after all, a loving God who wanted the very best for His people!

MRS. MILLER: Well, country music wasn't always that way! I remember when "seldom was heard a discouraging word, and the skies were not cloudy all day."

DOUGLAS MILLER: Get real, Mom! Times have changed!

DR. GERALDOMAN: Maybe all this goes to show you that we shouldn't be so judgmental of each other's music! Maybe our young people are right—music doesn't really adversely influence anyone! We'll be right back after this commercial message.

ANNOUNCER: Listen to a letter recently sent to Deno's Donut Shop. "Dear Deno: For years I've felt lethargic and lazy, melancholic, and lonesome. I even thought of giving up on life. But then I discovered your special donuts! Since then my life has not been the same! I'm no longer tired all the time; now there doesn't seem to be enough time for all the stuff I want to do. I'm no longer melancholic and lonesome. Now I have more friends than I know what to do with. Whenever I feel lazy and lethargic, I scarf down one of your special donuts. My laziness loses its grip on me, and my lethargy turns to luminous activity. Deno, thanks. I couldn't live without your donuts. Lovingly, Lydia." There you are folks, one more glowing testimonial. Why not stop on your way to work tomorrow morning and experience the power of Deno's Donuts?

DR. GERALDOMAN: We're back. Well, I guess it's time to hear from the audience. Who has a question today?

(STUDIO GUEST raises her hand.)

STUDIO GUEST: Dr. Geraldoman, it's obvious you don't think what we listen to adversely influences us. Is that right?

DR. GERALDOMAN *(laughs):* I guess you might say that.

STUDIO GUEST: Well, if you really believe that, why does Deno's Donuts spend $500,000 for a 30-second commercial spot on your show? It seems to me, using your logic, we should inform Deno's Donuts that they're wasting their money.

DR. GERALDOMAN: Hardly! My research has shown that commercials work. Every dollar spent on advertising comes back in increased sales—and then some!

STUDIO GUEST: So, doesn't it stand to reason that if advertising influences us, so will music?

DR. GERALDOMAN: Um … Well, that's all the time we have today! Sorry, we aren't able to field more questions. We thank our guests for sharing their thoughts with us! Be sure to tune in tomorrow when we'll be hearing from lawyers who defend the rights of mass murderers.

(Aside) This has been one tough show! I need to go to Deno's Donut Shop now, for one of Deno's special "pick me up" donuts!

Unless otherwise indicated, Scripture quotations: NIV®
© 1995 CPH

11 Whom Do You Admire Most and Why?

Focus

As human beings we often put our sports heroes and favorite movie stars on pedestals, making them almost godlike. Though it is not wrong to have heroes, it is sinful when we allow these heroes to direct our attention away from God and His ways. Because we often lose focus, Jesus Christ became our hero by going to the cross, dying for our sins, and rescuing us from sin, death, and the power of the devil.

Objectives

As a result of the Holy Spirit working through the Word the students will

1. acknowledge that their heroes are fallible;
2. confess that because of their heroes they sometimes lose perspective and may even do things contrary to God's will;
3. give thanks for Jesus Christ, the real hero of humankind.

A Powerful Word for the Leader

For additional perspective on this topic a devotional study is available for the leader. It is "Heroes," unit 2, study 11, found in *Power Words: Devotional Studies for Youth Bible Study Leaders*, CPH 20-2629.

This Study at a Glance

Activity	Time	Materials
An Ideal Hero	10 minutes	Newsprint and markers
A Perfect Hero	20 minutes	Bibles
Who's Your Hero?	20 minutes	Six copies of power play 11, copies of student page 12
Thanking a Hero	10 minutes	

An Ideal Hero

Invite the students to divide into groups of three to four. Give each group a sheet of newsprint and markers. Ask members of the group to appoint one person to take notes or create a drawing. Tell them to describe the perfect hero in words or in a picture. Ask, "What makes a person a hero? What does he or she look like? What does she do? What does he think or say? What other attributes make him or her a hero?" After a few minutes of brainstorming, invite each group to report its descriptions. Post them for all to see.

Ask, "In what ways are our heroes alike?"

A Perfect Hero

Ask the students to look up the request made by James and John in Mark 10:35–45. Invite a volunteer to read the story aloud. Then ask the students, "What did James and John want when they asked to sit next to Jesus in His glory?" (They were asking for positions of prestige and power. They wanted "hero" status.)

Remind the students that the expression to "drink the [same] cup" meant to share someone's fate. Jesus' fate was to die for the sins of humankind. Though James and John would not and could not pay the price for the sins of any person, they did undoubtedly suffer in their lifetime. Yet, Jesus did not grant their request to sit at His right or left side, because such a decision belonged exclusively to God His Father. Only the Father, Jesus said, has authority to determine who sits in the places of honor. (See Matthew 20:23.)

Discuss the following questions.

1. Although James and John wanted positions of greatness, what, according to Jesus, truly makes someone great? (Greatness is in servanthood, being humble, and giving in loving service.)

2. Why was Jesus a perfect hero? (See 1 Peter 2:22–24 and Revelation 5:12. He humbly "bore our sins in His body on the tree, so that we might die to sins and live for righteousness." Thus, He is worthy of all our praise.)

Now ask the students to compare their original description of a hero, which they drew up at the beginning of the lesson, with a picture of the perfect hero, Jesus Christ. Ask the following questions.

1. Is their ideal picture of a hero similar to the perfect picture of the hero, Jesus Christ? In what ways is it quite different?

2. According to Jesus, do heroes really have to look a certain way? sound a certain way? (Heroes will only look a certain way in that they will be seen doing God's work, serving, often quietly behind the scenes, in order to carry out God's purpose.)

3. According to Jesus, what truly makes a person great? (A humble, gentle spirit of service.)

4. Once more, define the word *hero*. As the students define the word, jot down their definitions on the chalkboard. Work through the different definitions and come up with one on which you can all agree.

Who's Your Hero?

Then say, "Let's see how our definition matches up with the opinions of people on the street." Present the power play.

Distribute copies of student page 12. Work together to record a definition of a hero on which everyone can agree. Below the definition ask each student to name a person in his or her life who has some "heroic" characteristics and to list the things that make this person a hero.

Then refer the students to the quotations from the play. Ask them to cross out those things stated by different characters in the play that do not match their defintion of a hero. Underline those things that do match the definition.

Thanking a Hero

Close with a prayer of thanks for the perfect hero, Jesus Christ. In your prayer incorporate the words of Revelation 5:12, "Worthy is the Lamb [our hero], who was slain, to receive power and wealth and wisdom and strength and honor and glory and praise!"

Provide writing paper and ask the students to write a letter to their parents about how much they are appreciated. Encourage the students to use the word *hero* in their description of their mom or dad. Invite them to deliver this letter at an appropriate time this week. Challenge them to decide on a way to show their appreciation.

Heroes

A hero is …

My hero is …

The qualities that make this person my hero are …

From "Who's Your Hero?"

"[My heroine] stands for the same things I do. She wants to save the whales, and she's gotten Congress to put aside millions to do it. She has also gotten tough on those pro-lifers!"

"I'm my own hero! … I am asked to speak all over the world, especially at high school assemblies. I tell these kids how they can turn their skinny bodies into a great body like mine! I tell them that they don't have to worry about bullies shoving them around. When you're a hunk of muscle like me, you can be king of the mountain. Men envy me, and women can't resist me."

"Actually, my hero is my mom. She's my hero because she has always been real … no facade … no pretense … no phoniness. When my dad left her for another woman, she picked up the pieces and went on with her life! My dad sort of forgot about me along with Mom, but Mom never forgot about me. She demonstrated character and consistency. I have always known she loves me, and through her teaching, I have learned that God loves me as well. My mom is my hero and role model."

© 1995 CPH

Power Plays 2, Student Page 12

Power Play 11

Who's Your Hero?

(Six copies of this script are needed.)

For even the Son of Man did not come to be served, but to serve, and to give His life as a ransom for many. (Mark 10:45)

Summary

Heroes don't look or sound a certain way. Usually real heroes don't even know they're heroes. You might even find one in your own mirror.

Characters

- INTERVIEWER—a reporter for KPWR television station
- VIDEO PERSON—someone who tapes the interviews with a video camera
- LARRY—a busy-looking man
- DELORES—a young business woman
- MARCUS—an award-winning body builder
- FLORINDA—a shopper

Setting

A busy sidewalk

Props (Optional)

- A note pad for the interviewer
- Video recorder
- A gym bag

INTERVIEWER: Good morning, KPWR viewers. Recently, we've seen several major figures in sports, politics, and the media discredited. Our heroes have let us down. Today, we're out on the street to ask people who their heroes are and what makes these people heroes. *(LARRY enters stage right.)* Okay, here comes someone right now! *(To LARRY)* I'm from KPWR television station. Could you tell me your name, and who your hero is?

LARRY: What business is it of yours? Buzz off!

(INTERVIEWER is taken aback a bit but composes self as DELORES enters stage left.)

INTERVIEWER: Excuse me. I'm from KPWR television station, and I'm wondering if you have a moment to answer a few questions.

DELORES: Sure.

INTERVIEWER: What's your name?

DELORES: My name is Delores.

INTERVIEWER: Delores, I'm wondering if you have a hero, and could you tell us why he or she is your hero?

DELORES *(thinks for a few seconds)*: Yes, I have a hero. Actually, you might say she's a heroine. She's our Senator—Hilda Linton. Hilda is my kind of lady. She stands for the same things I do. She wants to save the whales, and she's gotten Congress to put aside millions to do it. She has also gotten tough on those pro-lifers! Who do those people think they are carrying signs in front of abortion clinics? Those poor women have enough worries carrying around unwanted babies without some fanatics making them feel guilty! You know, I hope Mrs. Linton gets reelected this year!

INTERVIEWER: So, just how would you define a hero or heroine?

DELORES: A heroine is someone who fights for what's right and does it for unselfish reasons!

INTERVIEWER: Thank you. Oh, here comes someone with his gym bag. Gee, it looks like Marcus McCoy, the award-winning body builder. This should be interesting. Sir, I'm from KPWR television station, and I'm wondering if I could ask you a few questions?

MARCUS: Sure thing!

73

INTERVIEWER: You're the famous Marcus McCoy, body-building champion. Tell me, just who is your hero, and what makes him or her a hero?

MARCUS: Well (gives a body-builder's stance), actually, I'm my own hero!

INTERVIEWER (taken aback a bit): Yes, I guess you are a hero! I must confess you certainly look like a hero.

MARCUS: I know! I have won many awards in the last 10 years, some of which I'm sure you've heard of.

INTERVIEWER: Yes, I do recall reporting on those awards to my audience. Why don't you review for us some of the more famous awards you've received.

MARCUS: Of course! Last month I received the coveted Mr. Macho Body-Building Champion Award, and just last week I won the Mr. Galaxy Competition. I am asked to speak all over the world, especially at high school assemblies. I tell these kids how they can turn their skinny bodies into a great body like mine! I tell them that they don't have to worry about bullies shoving them around. When you're a hunk of muscle like me, you can be king of the mountain. Men envy me, and women can't resist me. But let's be honest: physical beauty is not everything. My outward appearance reflects the spiritually and emotionally beautiful person I am inside!

INTERVIEWER: Well, I see. You certainly do sound like a hero!

MARCUS: It's true. I like to think, "What looks like a hero and sounds like a hero is more than likely a hero."

INTERVIEWER (sarcastically): I can see why you might think that way! Thank you.

MARCUS: It was my pleasure to share some of my charm and greatness with you.

INTERVIEWER: We have time for just one more person on the street to tell us about his or her hero. Here comes someone right now. Excuse me. Could you tell me who your hero is and why?

FLORINDA: Yeah. I guess so. Actually, my hero is my mom. She's my hero because she has always been real ... no facade ... no pretense ... no phoniness. When my dad left her for another woman, she picked up the pieces and went on with her life! My dad sort of forgot about me along with Mom, but Mom never forgot about me. She demonstrated character and consistency. I have always known she loves me, and through her teaching, I have learned that God loves me as well. My mom is my hero and my role model.

INTERVIEWER: Well, that's certainly a nice tribute to your mother. Do you think she knows she's a hero?

FLORINDA: No, I don't think real heroes know they're heroes.

INTERVIEWER: Are you saying that heroes don't look or sound a certain way?

FLORINDA: Yes, I guess I am. I'm saying heroes can live next door. They can live in your house! In fact, a hero might be found the next time you look in your own mirror!

INTERVIEWER: Thanks. Well folks, you've heard a variety of opinions on heroes today. What do you think? Who's your hero?

Peace of Mind in Violent Times

This Study at a Glance

Activity	Time	Materials
Violent Times	10 minutes	Copies of student page 13
Violence	15 minutes	Three copies of power play 12
God's Word	15 minutes	Bibles
God's Word at Work	10 minutes	
*Closing	10 minutes	Paraphrase of Psalm 46 from previous activity

Advance preparation or special supplies required.

Violent Times

Distribute copies of student page 13. Direct the students to complete the student page. Discuss their responses. Point out that violence is a very real part of the world and of their lives. Their reactions to violence may range from fear to denial to resistance. Discuss which reaction is more effective. Jesus' disciples had problems with violence too. Introduce the play.

Violence

Read the Scripture verse (Luke 9:51–55) to set the stage for the power play. Then watch the play with the class. Afterward, discuss how easy it was for the three disciples to slip into violent modes of behavior. Ask, "Why is it so easy to get mad?" (Violence is a part of our human nature. [See Matthew 15:19.])

Make a list on the board or a sheet of newsprint of the things that make people in the group mad. "How do you react to these factors? Does a violent reaction help?" (Answers will vary.)

Then ask, "Is it wrong to be angry?" (Sometimes anger may be an appropriate response if it does not result in sinful behavior.

Focus

We live in a violent world. Our fear of danger all around us is surpassed only by our fear of the violence lying within us. Yet, God has brought peace to our world in the sacrificial death of His Son. God's promise to protect us from violence and evil is strong and sure. Because of Jesus Christ, we are able to live in peace with God, with ourselves, and with others.

Objectives

By the power of Christ at work in them through the Spirit the students will

1. recognize the ways violence shows itself in their world and in their lives;
2. feel confident of God's protection and of His ability to deal with the violence they face;
3. live at peace in this world with themselves and with others.

A Powerful Word for the Leader

For additional perspective on this topic a devotional study is available for the leader. It is "Our Violent God?" unit 2, study 12, found in *Power Words: Devotional Studies for Youth Bible Study Leaders*, CPH 20-2629.

God's Word

Divide the class into small groups. Assign each group one of the following Bible references: Genesis 4:1–16; Genesis 34:1–29; Judges 16:20–31; and 2 Samuel 11:14–26. Ask group members to answer the following questions:

1. Who was violent?
2. Why?
3. What was the result?
4. How did the people involved feel about the violence?

Let a representative of each group share their findings with the entire class.

Suggested responses to the Bible references are as follows:

Genesis 4:1–16—(1) Cain; (2) jealousy; (3) he was banished; (4) fear. Also, God was angry with Cain and threatened punishment upon anyone who harmed Cain. In this case, God's righteous anger caused Cain to depend on Him and be less afraid of the violence of others.

Genesis 34:1–29—(1) Shechem, Simeon, and Levi; (2) passion, revenge; (3) Shechem's death, judgment upon Simeon and Levi (Genesis 49:5–7); (4) indifference, grief, and fury (v. 7).

Judges 16:20–31—(1) Samson, the Philistines; (2) the Philistines gouged out Samson's eyes and humiliated him; (3) Samson killed his enemies when he pulled down the pillars; revenge—many of God's enemies were destroyed; and death for Samson; (4) fear, anger, revenge, faith on Samson's part.

2 Samuel 11:14–26—(1) David; (2) he wanted Uriah killed so he could have Uriah's wife; (3) Uriah died in battle, and David married Bathsheba; (4) guilt.

Jesus focused the full force of His love and power on the real enemy—Satan—and destroyed the author of violence and evil. Now, although violence is still a reality in our world and must be dealt with, it has no real power over us. The truth is Jesus is Lord, and He is in control of our past, present, and future.

Direct the class to turn to Psalm 46. Have the class find references to tumultuous acts or events referred to in the psalm. (The earth gives way, mountains fall into the sea, waters roar, mountains quake, nations in uproar, kingdoms fall, desolation, wars.)

Discuss the following questions.

1. In the face of this frightening scenario, who is in control? (God.)
2. What is God doing while this violence is occurring? (He is always there—a fortress in the midst of chaos. He controls the forces of nature as well as the acts of human beings.)

3. The first verse says He is "our refuge and strength." Who is meant by "our"? (God's people. That means you and your students—all for whom Christ has died. By the power of the Holy Spirit, we are a part of His family by grace through faith. As God protected His people in years past, He is with us today too.)

God's Word at Work

1. Ask, "Have you or has anyone you know ever been the victim of an act of violence? Name some real threats you face each day." (Gangs, family violence, kidnapping, auto accidents, possibility of war.) "How do you protect yourself against them?" (Answers will vary. Help students formulate practical responses as time allows.)

2. Ask, "How do you control your anger when you are tempted to lose your temper?" (List helpful techniques—prayer, counting to 10, walking away from the situation temporarily, talking it out.)

3. Ask the students to name three violent movies or songs with violent lyrics. "Does watching these movies or listening to this music influence you in any way? Does it cause you to act more violently? Have you become complacent about the tragic consequences of violence?"

Closing

Write the outline that follows on the board or on newsprint so all can see. Do this in advance so all you have to do in class is complete each line. Working together, write a paraphrase of portions of Psalm 46 by completing each line.

God is our refuge and strength, an everpresent …

Therefore we will not fear, though …

God will help [His people] at …

Nations are …

He lifts His voice, the …

The LORD Almighty is with us; the God of …

is our …

Come and see the works of the LORD. He …

Be still, and know that I am God; I will be exalted among …

The God of …

is our …

Speak together the paraphrase of Psalm 46 you have created. At the end, add prayers for specific needs as identified by students—especially for the safety of friends and family.

Extending the Lesson

Look at these additional stories of violence within Scripture and discuss: (1) Who is violent? (2) Why? (3) What are the results of the violence? (4) How did the people involved feel about the violence?

- Genesis 37:12–36
- Judges 19:1–30
- Acts 6:8–15
- Acts 7:54–60

Find examples of violence in today's news. Analyze them in the same way: Who? Why? Result? Feeling?

Find examples of nonviolence in today's newspaper.

Violent Times

1. How do you feel about the topic of violence? (Circle the letter of your choice.)

    a. I'm tired of hearing about it.

    b. It scares me.

    c. What violence?

    d. _____

2. Which of the following statements summarizes your opinion about the best way to react when faced with a confrontation?

    a. Peace at any price.

    b. The end justifies the means.

    c. Look the other way.

    d. _____

3. What would be worth fighting for?

    a. My money.

    b. My CD collection.

    c. My family.

    d. My life.

    e. _____

    f. Nothing.

4. Rate yourself by writing "Me" somewhere on the following grid, with passive being #1 and aggressive being #10.

    1_____10

5. Rate Jesus with a cross on the same scale.

    1_____10

Power Play 12

Violence

(Three copies of this script are needed.)

As the time approached for Him to be taken up to heaven, Jesus resolutely set out for Jerusalem. And He sent messengers on ahead, who went into a Samaritan village to get things ready for Him; but the people there did not welcome Him, because He was heading for Jerusalem. When the disciples James and John saw this, they asked, "Lord, do You want us to call fire down from heaven to destroy them?" But Jesus turned and rebuked them. (Luke 9:51–55)

Summary

Violence is on the rise in our society today, but reports of violence certainly were common in Jesus' time too. In this play we look in on James and John, two disciples who were called the "Sons of Thunder." They are joined by another disciple, Peter, well-known for his "leap-before-you-look" approach to life. We see James and John shortly after they have been rebuked by Jesus (Luke 9).

Characters

JAMES, JOHN, PETER—disciples of Jesus

Setting

An imaginary encounter between the disciples. This play would work well in an outdoor setting. JAMES and JOHN are angrily conversing. PETER is sitting in the background listening.

JAMES *(obviously angry):* I don't understand Jesus. Those Samaritans deserved to be slaughtered after what they did.

JOHN *(also angry):* He could have wiped them out in an instant. I can't believe they had the guts to treat us that way—especially Jesus.

JAMES: Well, we could have gone to the east of the Jordan, but no! He has to march right through Samaria to a hostile town. Sometimes He scares me. What is He trying to prove?

JOHN: If He wants people to understand God's power, it seems like a little fire from heaven wouldn't be too far out of line. That would really get their attention!

JAMES: Well, at least, a few seconds before the fire fried them!

JOHN: I'd like to see the entire country wiped out. What do we need Samaritans for anyway?

JAMES: I don't know, but Jesus seems to think they're worth saving!

JOHN: That makes one of us!

JAMES: Speaking of Jesus, I'm still trying to figure out why He got so mad at us. The minute I suggested calling fire down from heaven to destroy them, He went through the roof!

JOHN: He just doesn't understand good strategy.

JAMES: We'll just get pushed around if we don't show how strong we are.

(PETER has been moving toward them during the last few lines of dialog.)

PETER: I can't believe you guys! You just don't get it! How long have you two been with Jesus? You still don't have a clue as to what He's all about.

JOHN: And I suppose you do!

PETER: I sure understand a lot more than you do!

JAMES: You know, Peter, I am tired of your attitude. I remember a time when your faith was in the pits. Remember that, John, when he tried to walk on the water to Jesus?

JOHN: You mean the time he ... *(JOHN motions his hand downward)* when he should have ... *(JOHN then motions his hand upward; he and JAMES both laugh.)*

79

JAMES: You talk big, Peter, but you're not so great. Don't be giving us advice. At least, we didn't look foolish out on that lake!

PETER: I tripped.

JOHN: On the water? Give me a break!

JAMES: Oh, you of little faith! *(He and JOHN both laugh again.)*

PETER: You think you're so smart. I can think of a few times when you messed up too. Like arguing about who was going to be the greatest in God's kingdom. Like it could be either of you. You guys are real dunderheads.

JOHN: Speaking of heads, why don't you just go soak yours in a well or something!

PETER *(becoming really angry):* You know, I've had just about enough of you. *(He moves toward JOHN as if he is going to strike him. JAMES grabs his arm.)*

JAMES: You want to fight, fight me. You always try to pick on John because he's smaller than you.

PETER: It's not my fault he has a big mouth and a short body!

JOHN: Oh yeah? I could beat you with one hand tied behind my back. *(The three of them start to push each other. As they scuffle, an object falls out of PETER's pocket. Suddenly they all stand still and look at the object on the ground.)*

JOHN: What's that?

PETER *(reaching down and picking it up):* Nothing, just a rock.

JAMES: You carry a rock with you? Why?

PETER *(becoming very quiet and serious):* Remember how stormy it was the day when I walked out on the water to Jesus? Well, after I sank, I was feeling really stupid and discouraged. When we got back to shore, I noticed this rock lying in the water with the waves washing over it. It was smooth where the water had worn it down.

JOHN: So?

PETER: When I picked it up, I thought about what Jesus had said to us about building on something solid. I remembered as I was sinking in the ocean, with the storm all around me, the look in His eyes. Somehow I knew that what I saw there was all I would ever need for the rest of my life.

JAMES: What do you mean?

PETER: He had that calm certainty while the whole world was in turmoil around me. The love and compassion and forgiveness that were there in that one look … *(He pauses.)* I can't really explain it.

JOHN: So, I still don't understand. Why the stone?

PETER: You guys know me. I shoot my mouth off before I think. I'm not the brightest guy in the world. Look where we were a few minutes ago, all of us fighting and yelling.

JAMES *(looking sheepish):* Yeah, sorry about that!

PETER: But things like that happen. Misunderstandings, fighting, wars, they are all a part of life.

JOHN: What about the rock?

PETER: I figured that if anybody has rough edges, it's got to be me. It reminds me of Jesus, in His gentle way, continually smoothing out my rough edges. He teaches us the same things over and over. Look how smooth the rock is where the waves have washed over it again and again. I just keep it, well, I keep it because …

JAMES: I'm beginning to understand.

PETER: Jesus has amazing patience with us. Let's be more patient with each other. Okay?

JOHN: Peter, I guess we all are a little thick headed. Jesus keeps telling us to love each other, and we keep fighting and complaining! You'd think we'd learn, wouldn't you?

PETER: Maybe we will yet! Come on, we've got a long walk ahead!